Just
chocolate

Just chocolate

**Rich and luscious recipes for
cakes, biscuits, desserts and treats**

Kathryn Hawkins

NEW
HOLLAND

First published in 2008 by New Holland Publishers (UK) Ltd
London • Cape Town • Sydney • Auckland
Text and recipe copyright © 2008 Kathryn Hawkins
Photographs copyright © 2008 New Holland Publishers (UK) Ltd
Copyright © 2008 New Holland Publishers (UK) Ltd

Garfield House, 86–88 Edgware Road, London W2 2EA
www.newhollandpublishers.com

80 McKenzie Street, Cape Town 8001, South Africa
Unit 1, 66 Gibbes Street, Chatswood, NSW 2067, Australia
218 Lake Road, Northcote, Auckland, New Zealand

ISBN 978 1 84773 233 0

Commissioning editor: Clare Sayer Copy-editor: Clare Hubbard
Design: Glyn Bridgewater Photography: Stuart West Food styling: Katie Rogers
Production: Marion Storz Editorial Direction: Rosemary Wilkinson

Reproduction by Pica Digital PTE Ltd, Singapore
Printed and bound by Tien Wah Press, Malaysia

10 9 8 7 6 5 4 3 2 1

NOTE The author and publishers have made every effort to ensure that all instructions given in this book are safe and accurate, but they cannot accept liability for any resulting injury or loss or damage to either property or person, whether direct or consequential and howsoever arising.

- Both metric and imperial measures are given in the recipes – follow either set of measures but not a mixture of both as they are not interchangeable.

- Oven temperatures are given for conventional ovens. If using a fan oven, reduce the oven temperature by 20°C (70°F).

- Due to the slight risk of salmonella, children, the elderly and pregnant women should avoid recipes with lightly cooked or raw eggs.

- Medium eggs should be used unless otherwise stated.

Contents

Introduction

Chocolate is as popular as ever; there have never been as many varieties as there are today. I've never met anyone who doesn't like chocolate. In my experience you either love it or you really love it! For me, the best way to enjoy chocolate is in the form of a piece of gooey chocolate fudge cake, washed down with a cup of coffee. It's an indulgent, sweet treat, to which nothing else comes remotely close. As children, my brother and I were only allowed chocolate on special occasions and I still regard it as such today. When my grandparents came to visit us they always brought us chocolate, but we were only allowed to have some if we ate up all our lunch. Funnily enough, our lunch was always gobbled down! When we spent our pocket money on sweets I remember that milk or white chocolate mice and chocolate buttons covered in hundreds and thousands were a 'must have' in our sweetie bags, and an ice-cream cornet just wasn't the same without a chocolate flake stuck in the top. Some of my happiest childhood days were a special outing followed by a chocolate treat for good behaviour. We have a marvellous photograph of my brother typifying such an occasion – his mouth and hands are smothered in chocolate and he looks blissfully happy, his face lit up with a broad chocolatey smile.

The great thing about chocolate for me, as a cookery writer, is that it's so versatile. Apart from being a delicious morsel to eat and enjoy on its own, chocolate can be used in baking,

confectionery, hot and cold puddings, sauces, frostings, piped as decorations and in drinks – the list is endless. It's an excellent subject for a recipe book because you can make so many things with it, as you will find out. Chocolate has a fascinating history and you'll discover its almost mythical story in the first few pages of this book. It is also reputed to have all sorts of effects on the body and psyche, so I've included a few chocolate facts for you to enjoy. You'll find all you need to know about using chocolate in your cooking, as well as notes on the different varieties on the market today and lots of ideas for using chocolate to further enhance your creations. The recipes are divided into chapters for easy reference and you'll find plenty of traditional favourites alongside more contemporary ideas. I use a whole range of chocolate varieties in my recipes from the lightest, creamiest white to the darkest, most intense, unsweetened chocolate. At the back of the book, you'll find a list of famous chocolatiers who have made a living out of their love of chocolate. Their work is highly innovative, and they use the best quality chocolate available and subsequently can demand high prices for their produce. It's worth sampling some of their products – pure bliss.

It's been so much fun tasting and cooking with all the different types of chocolate and extremely interesting working out which varieties suit specific recipes and flavourings. I hope you enjoy trying out my recipes for yourself, friends and family. Now I need to go on a diet...

Story of chocolate

Cocoa originates from the New World. The Mexican Olmec people were the first to cultivate the cocoa tree, and it was adopted by the Mayans sometime before 600 BC. The Maya people grew cocoa in Central America and, in turn, traded it to the Aztecs. The Aztecs developed cocoa as a product by roasting and grinding the beans and turning it into a drink. It was such a valuable commodity to them that they used the beans as currency.

The wider world learnt of this great product from Christopher Columbus who, on his fourth voyage in 1502, brought some back to Spain. He and his entourage told stories of the Aztec's rituals and recipes. The Aztec emperor, Montezuma, would indulge in a bitter chocolate drink flavoured with chillies and spices, served in gold goblets, and taken as an aphrodisiac. The drink was called xocolatl, meaning 'bitter water'. Aztec soldiers and dignitaries would drink it after a meal, by grinding a block of cocoa into hot water. Although bitter-tasting, it was reported as being refreshing and satisfying. The Aztec flavourings were soon adopted by the Spanish, and as word spread throughout Europe, cocoa concoctions began to include sugar, nuts, spices and flower waters.

The first European cocoa factory opened in Spain in 1580, and it produced a spicy paste. In France and England the added ingredients were stripped back to vanilla and sugar only, and by the late seventeenth century this simple mixture was sold as a hot

drink made up with milk, in all the trendy Parisian and London coffee houses of the day. The first French factory opened in Bayonne in the eighteenth century and sold cocoa to companies in Paris and beyond.

The Spanish spread cocoa cultivation to Africa. From Mexico, cocoa was exported to the Philippines and cultivation was extended throughout the East Indies by the Dutch. Colonial Americans obtained cocoa from the West Indies and by the late seventeenth century it was enjoyed there as a hot drink. Cocoa production began in North America in 1765 when Dr James Baker opened a small mill in Massachusetts and entered the business. In 1828 in the Netherlands, Van Houten unveiled a press that extracted more cocoa butter than ever before. The resulting cocoa was smoother and finer and was easier to mix with liquid; it was called Dutch cocoa powder. The press led to the development of techniques we associate today with chocolate-making and by the mid-1800s, the first solid chocolate bars were developed in England by the Cadbury brothers and Fry & Sons, and the chocolate industry was born. In 1876, Daniel Peter of Switzerland presented the first milk chocolate bar to the world, and a couple of years later, another Swiss producer, Lindt, started producing finer quality chocolates.

At the turn of the twentieth century in the USA, Milton Hershey invented the Hershey bar and pointed the way for other manufacturers to follow. Throughout the century chocolate was increasingly consumed by the masses, turning chocolate into a multi-billion dollar global industry. Chiefly, the majority of the chocolate eaten was in the form of sweetened candy bars, but Lindt continued producing finer chocolate and catered for the more sophisticated palate. By the 1970s interest in darker chocolate for cooking and eating grew, and there was a fascination for discovering the roots of chocolate and seeking out original Aztec flavourings.

Today chocolate has reached new heights as a gourmet food. It is promoted by specialist clubs and societies, tastings are conducted and chocolate is appreciated in the same way as fine wine. A professional chocolatier will listen for the sharp 'snapping' sound of good quality chocolate, and their nose will detect notes of flower essences, fruits, balsam and green tea. The Internet has meant that we have easy access to chocolates from all over the world enabling us to taste the most delicious flavours, in often outrageous shapes, flavoured with fine liqueurs, champagne and decorated with gold leaf. (See page 186 for a list of some of the world's finest chocolate-makers.)

Chocolate is a crowd-wooer and show-stopper. A chocolate fountain is a real 'must have' for many parties these days – who can resist the molten, rippling chocolate as it flows seductively. However, for me, it's satisfying to know, that any celebration or get-together can still be halted by the arrival of a chocolate cake. I've made chocolate wedding cakes for both my brother and my best friend and I can remember being showered with compliments from everyone on how lovely it was to have a chocolate cake instead of the more traditional fruit one. It seems our love for this ancient food grows stronger... let's hope it stays that way.

Feelgood factor

As we have already discovered, the Aztecs had already recognized the uplifting properties of cocoa, both as an aphrodisiac and a stimulant. Soon after cocoa was introduced to France, it began to be used by the medics as a cure for fevers and chest and stomach disorders, and it was widely sold in apothecaries in the eighteenth and nineteenth centuries. In the UK, the Quaker families of Cadbury, Fry, Terry and Rowntree all advertized cocoa powder as a healthy alternative to gin, claiming that it was a restorative health tonic for the working classes, not just for the food society's elite. This might all seem a little strange to us today, but you can see that these are clearly the foundations for some of our modern-day thoughts and notions about chocolate.

In the twenty-first century, we tend to be bombarded with health reports and conflicting information, so here are some solid chocolate facts:

- Cocoa beans, like all beans, are rich in nutrients because they support the germination of a plant. They are rich in the antioxidant vitamin E and the super antioxidants – flavonoids. These help reduce the build-up of blood cholesterol on the artery walls. Remember though, high cocoa solids means high antioxidants, but the addition of milk, sugar or cocoa butter dilutes these properties.

• Cocoa and chocolate are rich in saturated fat which is notorious for raising blood cholesterol. However, the type of saturated fat found in cocoa is peculiar in that the body is able to convert it into an unsaturated fat which actually lowers the risk of blood clotting which can lead to a heart attack. Once again, this refers to chocolate in its purest form, with a high cocoa content.

- Cocoa and chocolate contain two stimulants – theobromine and caffeine. The former is a weaker stimulant of the nervous system than caffeine. The amount of caffeine found in cocoa and chocolate is significantly lower than in tea and coffee. For example, 30g (1oz) cocoa contains 60mg caffeine; the same amount of unsweetened chocolate contains 30mg; milk chocolate contains even less. By comparison, a standard cup of instant coffee has about 80mg caffeine.

- Many people experience cravings for chocolate. It does contain very small amounts of substances that can affect the brain in a similar way to marijuana, and also phenylethylamine, a natural chemical with amphetamine-like effects. However, psychologists have carried out tests on patients who 'lust' after chocolate, and have shown that they can be just as satisfied after eating imitations containing no chocolate at all.

- Chocolate is very easy and pleasurable to eat. It melts quickly and smoothly on the tongue, providing great sensory pleasure, stimulating the taste buds and releasing 'happy' chemicals in the brain called endorphins. Combine these properties with the energy boost from the sugar and fat content, and this is probably more of an explanation for an individual's cravings and why so many people are seduced by it.

- Because chocolate is rich in fat, and sugar in some varieties, it is high in calories and good for a quick energy boost. It also contains protein and iron. This makes it essential survival food for soldiers and mountaineers.

Types of chocolate

When I was a little girl, in my innocence, I believed that there were only two types of chocolate: chocolate for mums and dads, and chocolate for children. Theirs was plain and ours was milk or white. A very simplistic formula, but the basic theory was vaguely correct, although I can now see that it was applied when my parents wanted to keep us away from their chocolate!

In reality, chocolate is available in many different forms, from powdered to solid block, in portions for easy baking or more refined bars for eating. All chocolate, even that of the same type, has its own taste due to differences in the location, quality, production and manufacturing of the cocoa beans used. Just like variations in types of tea and coffee, there are several different types of cocoa bean, and these are carefully blended to achieve the best flavour possible. Chocolate manufacturing is a complex process, but it's an interesting journey from the origins of a seed from the cacao tree to the finished product. I'm including a brief story of its production from start to finish.

Production of chocolate

The cacao is an evergreen tree native to Latin America that grows from 6–12 metres (20–40 feet) tall, depending on conditions. It requires shelter and protection as it grows, and this is usually supplied by banana or rubber trees. The flowers grow directly on the tree trunk, but only a few develop into the oval, melon-shaped pods that are either deep yellow or rich red in colour. The flowers and pods grow together throughout the year, but the pods are only harvested twice a year. When the pods are ripe, they are collected, split and the contents scraped out. The seeds or beans and surrounding pulp are left in the sun to help them ferment and in turn develop a good flavour. Once this has happened, the beans are dried and exported for processing.

On arrival at the factory, the beans are cleaned and then roasted to develop the flavour further and reduce the moisture content. The husks are removed, which leaves only the kernels or nibs – these are the vital parts of chocolate and cocoa manufacturing. They are ground into a paste and the heat produced by the grinding mechanism at this stage helps release the fat or cocoa butter. Once ground, the resulting chocolate mass becomes liquid and is known as chocolate liquor. When the liquor cools, it solidifies and becomes basic, unsweetened chocolate. It can then be processed further to make cocoa and other types of chocolate.

Cocoa powder

Chocolate liquor is pressed further to exude more cocoa butter, and then the residue is ground down to make the dry powder we know as cocoa. It is unsweetened and has a fat content between 10 and 35 per cent. Cocoa is used in baking and desserts and is sieved into mixtures to give a pure, intense chocolate flavour. It can also be mixed with sugar and hot milk to make a rich drink.

Drinking chocolate

Drinking chocolate or chocolate powder is specifically designed for mixing with hot milk and/or hot water to make a soothing drink or for sprinkling over cakes, desserts and frothy coffee. Some are made from chocolate powder with sugar, emulsifying agents and flavourings added; better quality varieties contain cocoa powder and grated chocolate. Other products also have dried milk powder added and are 'instant drinks', requiring only hot water to make them up. Because of the increased sugar and lower cocoa content, drinking chocolate is not a suitable substitute for cocoa powder.

Unsweetened/baker's chocolate

This is cooled chocolate liquor mixed with a quantity of cocoa butter, and can contain up to 95 per cent cocoa. It contains no sugar and is therefore very bitter and reddish-brown in colour. It grates and melts well and, like cocoa, it gives a full chocolate flavour. It is often packaged wrapped in individual 30g (1oz) squares. Popular in the USA and Canada, it can be difficult to obtain elsewhere, but I managed to buy some online from a New York supermarket. If you cannot find this type of chocolate you can either replace it with one of the very high percentage cocoa chocolates, at least 85 per cent, (see below), or make your own mixture by combining 3 level Tbsp cocoa powder with 15g (½oz) unsalted butter. This would replace 30g (1oz) unsweetened chocolate. Remember to adjust the sugar quantity in the recipe accordingly, if necessary.

High percentage cocoa dark chocolate

Ranging from 85–100 per cent cocoa, this type of chocolate is usually available from specialist suppliers, and is designed for the real chocolate connoisseur. It is primarily very bitter and the intense flavour is not for the faint-hearted. But if this is your taste, you'll find different varieties described as having specific qualities (much like ground coffee) depending on the beans used and the roasting process. It is glossy, smooth and has a clean 'snapping' sound when broken. This type of chocolate is mainly used in cooking for a full, rich flavour, although it is often an expensive alternative to other types.

Continental plain chocolate

This type of chocolate has lower cocoa solids than those listed previously – usually between 50–78 per cent – with sugar added to it. It gives a good flavour and is probably the most widely used variety. It is ideal for desserts and goes well with coffee. This sort of chocolate can be eaten on its own, although it is probably too rich for most people to eat more than a few squares at a time.

Plain chocolate

Much more suitable for eating, this is a chocolate with lower cocoa solids and more sugar. All plain chocolate sold in the EU must contain at least 30 per cent cocoa solids, and in the USA it must contain 35–50 per cent, but it may, in effect, have as little as 15 per cent chocolate liquor. Often the sugar content is quite high, so this may make it unsuitable for cooking; you will have to adjust the sugar content in the recipe to suit the chocolate's sweetness.

Milk chocolate

Milk chocolate contains powdered or condensed milk and sugar which makes it sweet, creamy and mild in flavour. It has a lower percentage of cocoa solids – typically about 20 per cent, although richer varieties are available. It is very popular for eating as a treat and most prepared chocolate confectionery bars are made from this type of chocolate.

White chocolate

Not strictly a chocolate because it is not made from cocoa beans. It is made from cocoa butter to which milk, sugar and vanilla have been added. A sign of good quality would be that the chocolate was made with 'natural' or 'pure' vanilla rather than 'flavouring'. It has the same texture as other types of chocolate, but is pale yellowy-white in colour and tastes very sweet and creamy. It can be used like other chocolate, but it is not really interchangeable with other types. It is often used in conjunction with a darker variety to give colour contrast. Special care should be taken when melting white chocolate as it is more sensitive to heat than other varieties (see pages 32 and 33). White chocolate is a very popular treat for children.

Flavoured chocolate

There are many varieties of flavoured chocolate bars on the market today, some, at the top end of the market, use natural flavours, while others may include artificial flavourings; when it comes to which one to choose, it's a matter of personal preference. Flavoured chocolate may not melt very well as it is made for eating on its own rather than cooking, but if the

chocolate is of good quality it may be used in baking and offers an additional flavour to your chosen recipe. Common flavours include vanilla, coffee, cinnamon, orange and mint.

Chocolate chips, beans, buttons and chunks

Available in white, milk and plain varieties, these are small pieces of chocolate specially designed for baking and adding to recipes, such as cookies and muffins, or for sprinkling over ice creams and desserts for that extra chocolate flavour. They melt easily, but do make sure the chocolate is good quality by checking the cocoa solid content. Some products are made without cocoa butter and have vegetable oil and stabilizers added to them instead; these products have a different taste and mouth-feel and are generally inferior, but they do offer a firmer set than baking chocolate when they are used in desserts and sauces. As an alternative, you could chop your preferred bar of chocolate into small pieces and use this instead of the ready-prepared pieces.

Couverture or covering chocolate

A high-quality chocolate, mainly used by professional chocolate-makers. This type of chocolate would be 'tempered' – a process necessary for fine chocolate making (see page 43). Couverture contains a high percentage of cocoa solids which gives it the really glossy finish that is an essential mark of excellence. Available in dark, plain, milk and white varieties, it is expensive and is available from specialist suppliers.

Compound chocolate

Not to be confused with the couverture chocolate mentioned above, this is an inferior chocolate product made from cocoa solids mixed with vegetable oil and flavourings. It is used for melting, but lacks real chocolate flavour and glossiness. Inexpensive and easy to use, it is available in plain, milk and white varieties.

Organic chocolate

With the increasing concern about the quality of food we consume, there has been a rise in the production of organic foods, and chocolate and cocoa products are now widely available with this certification. The principle behind organic food is that it should be produced without the use of genetically-modified crops, pesticides and artificial fertilizers. The term 'organic' on food labelling is controlled in law by governments or legislative organizations, and any food labelled as such must meet a strict set of standards. It's a matter of personal choice, but some people say the products taste better, as well as avoiding the unnecessary ingesting of artificial chemicals and additives.

Fairtrade® chocolate

The Fairtrade® mark is an independent consumer label that appears on certain products as a guarantee that disadvantaged producers in the developing world are getting a better deal. The producers receive a minimum price that covers the cost of sustainable production and an extra premium that is invested in social or economic development projects. Their working conditions are better, they have more control over their lives and the chance to improve life for their family and community. Chocolate and cocoa are products that can be produced in this way, and it is one of the most environmentally-friendly of all crops. Cocoa producers belonging to this scheme can be found in the Dominican Republic, Ghana and Belize. Look out for the label the next time you buy chocolate to help the development of this type of production.

Chocolate for special diets

The dietary restrictions that an individual has will determine the type of chocolate they can eat. If you have to avoid dairy food, then choose a dark chocolate variety, or cocoa powder, which has no added milk. For sugar-restricted diets, unsweetened chocolate or a high percentage cocoa chocolate may be suitable in cooking, as would cocoa powder. However, as these products are so bitter, they would probably be intolerable without added sweetness. Carob is often used as a chocolate alternative, but the flavour is more caramely. Carob is a bean from a Mediterranean tree, and unlike chocolate, carob contains little fat and no caffeine, so would be a suitable alternative if you are on a low-fat diet or are caffeine intolerant. Carob can be obtained in a powder like cocoa or in bars – with and without sugar, with dairy or soya milk, flavoured, or with fruit and nuts.

Enhancing the flavour of chocolate in your cooking

The Aztecs blended cocoa with spices, scented flowers and even chillies. Today, the most widely-used flavouring is vanilla, as it enhances both the aroma and flavour of many chocolate recipes.

Spices like cinnamon, nutmeg, allspice and star anise also combine well with chocolate. If you want to try something more exotic, infuse chocolate-laced liquids with lemon grass, kaffir lime and spicy red chilli. The Mexicans add unsweetened chocolate or cocoa powder to rich spicy beef stews to make an intensely-flavoured sauce. Fresh basil increases the balsam, pepperiness of dark chocolate and I've even tried the darkest of chocolates with salty blue cheese – the flavours are strangely similar! In baking and confectionery, popular additions are coffee, caramel, toffee, banana, mint, orange, lime and roasted nuts. If you use dark brown sugar in the mixture for cakes, muffins or brownies, or light brown sugar for cookies, you'll increase the moistness and 'gooey' texture of your finished recipe.

Choosing and storage tips

Chocolate that is fresh and in tip-top condition should be glossy and unblemished. Avoid any with a greyish tone or 'bloom' – white spots or small holes. In general, it is best to keep chocolate in its original wrapping, or in foil, and then in an airtight container Cocoa powder is best kept in its original tin or container as long as it is airtight. Store in a cool, dry place, about 18°C (64°F) – the kitchen cupboard should be fine – but not in the fridge unless it is very warm. If you do keep chocolate in the fridge, it is likely that a whitish film will appear on the surface, which is the cocoa butter resurfacing. Although it doesn't affect the chocolate in any other way, it does make the chocolate look unattractive.

Unsweetened and dark chocolate will keep for many months if stored correctly. Plain and milk varieties will keep for about a year, and white chocolate for 6–8 months, but always read 'best before' dates on the packaging to check. Humidity will shorten the shelf life of chocolate, and other incorrect storage conditions will cause the chocolate to 'bloom'. 'Sugar bloom' occurs when the chocolate becomes damp and some of the sugar starts to dissolve. When the chocolate dries off again the sugar is left on the surface, giving it a mouldy-white appearance. If chocolate gets too warm, the cocoa butter melts and forms greyish-white areas on the surface when it cools. Although bloom spoils the appearance of the chocolate, it doesn't affect the flavour and the chocolate can still be eaten, but it is probably best used in cooking.

Chocolate techniques

Chocolate very versatile and you can use it to make so many attractive decorations that add flavour and a touch of decadence to cakes, desserts and sweet treats. Here are a few ideas for special finishing touches so you can get the most from chocolate.

Melting chocolate

Chocolate melts at blood temperature so little heat is required to soften it. The conventional method for melting chocolate on its own is by using a double boiler system. The other method that is now used is heating it in a microwave oven. When melting chocolate with other ingredients, it is often necessary to use the direct heat method.

Double boiler Break the chocolate into pieces and either place in a double boiler saucepan or in a heatproof bowl. Place the boiler top or the bowl over a saucepan of hot water. Make sure that the base of the bowl doesn't touch the water. Gently heat; do not let the water boil or produce steam. Allow the chocolate to melt – the time this takes will depend on the thickness and the amount of chocolate used. Chocolate retains its shape as it melts, so it will need a gentle stir to make it smooth. Carefully remove the boiler top or bowl from the saucepan and wipe away the water droplets. It is vital that no water gets into the chocolate as it melts as this will cause the chocolate to irreversibly stiffen and separate, rendering it unusable.

Microwave oven   High percentage cocoa or unsweetened chocolate can be melted at 50 per cent or medium power in the microwave, while milk and white are better melted on 30 per cent or low power. Break the chocolate into pieces and place in a microwave-proof bowl. The time it will take to melt the chocolate will depend on the amount used, its thickness and the power of the oven. As a rough guide: 100g (3½oz) high percentage cocoa chocolate will take about 4 minutes to melt using a 650–700W microwave oven at 50 per cent power. The same amount of milk or white chocolate would take the same time at 30 per cent power. Adjust time and power according to your oven. Check the chocolate frequently to make sure it isn't burning – white chocolate is especially susceptible to scorching.

NOTE: chocolate melted in the microwave with liquid or fat may melt more quickly because of the higher fat content of the ingredients, so it is advisable to check more frequently.

Direct heat method   This is used when other ingredients require melting as well or when a hot amalgam of ingredients is needed – for example, in a hot chocolate sauce. Choose a heavy-based saucepan and melt the ingredients together over a very low heat, stirring frequently, until melted and smooth. Remove from the heat immediately. Don't be tempted to raise the heat otherwise the contents will burn and spoil.

Marbling

Marbling different types of chocolate together is one of the most stunning effects. You can either marble the icing or frosting on top of cakes and bakes (see Blondies on pages 94–95) or make a sheet of marbled chocolate for creating curls, cut-outs or chocolate cases. The basic principle is the same however you use the finished marbled chocolate.

Choose two or three contrasting colours of chocolate and melt in separate bowls (see page 32). Place alternate teaspoonfuls of the melted chocolate on the cake/bake if decorating, or on a board lined with baking parchment if making a sheet of marbled chocolate. Tap the tin on the work surface so that the chocolates merge together, then drag a skewer through the chocolates to create a marbled effect. Tap again to smooth the chocolate and allow to set according to your recipe.

Chocolate curls

There are several ways to make curls of chocolate.

Quick curls Use a thick bar of chocolate that's been stored at room temperature. Hold the chocolate over a large plate or board lined with baking parchment, and use a swivel-headed vegetable peeler to 'peel' firmly along the edge of the chocolate, allowing the curls to fall on the plate or parchment. Place on a plate, lined with baking parchment and chill until required.

Caraque curls Melt the chocolate (see page 32) and spread it in a thin layer on to a marble slab or clean, smooth chopping board. Leave in a cool place until firm, but not hard (try to avoid refrigerating unless it is very warm). Draw a sharp, thin-bladed knife at a slight angle across the chocolate, using a slight sawing movement, scraping off thin layers to form long thin scrolls. Place on a plate lined with baking parchment and chill until required. This technique takes some practice! Store as for Quick curls (see page 35).

Chunky curls Prepare the chocolate as for caraque curls (see above). Drag a cheese slicer over the surface to form thick, curled scrolls. Store as before.

Piping chocolate and piped decorations

Iced cakes can be finished with simple chocolate piping. Melt the chocolate (see page 32) and spoon into a small, ready-made piping bag. Pipe tiny dots, double lines or shapes like hearts and flowers on to small cakes. For a contemporary look for a large cake, pipe the word 'chocolate' randomly over the top. You can use chocolate piping to make a number of other decorations.

Scribbles Have fun making your own freehand piped chocolate designs. Line a large baking sheet or chopping board with baking parchment. Melt the chocolate (see page 32) and spoon it into a small ready-made piping bag. Drizzle the chocolate in small, self-contained lattice designs, such as hearts, circles and squares. Allow to set firm before carefully peeling from the paper. Store as before.

Feathering Either spread the top of the cake with white glacé icing or melted white chocolate, then pipe straight lines of darker melted chocolate across the cake. Before the chocolate sets, draw a skewer through the lines; turn the cake round and draw the skewer in the opposite direction. Continue until the top is completely 'feathered'. You can also use piped white chocolate on a dark chocolate topping (see page 34). Place on a plate, line with baking parchment and chill until required.

Filigree scrolls Line a large baking sheet or chopping board with baking parchment. Pipe a random, self-contained, mesh-like design in an oblong shape, approximately 5 x 15cm (2 x 6in). Bring the short ends of the baking parchment towards each other, chocolate inside, and chill in this position, carefully wedged between two containers until set. Peel the paper away and use as a stunning centrepiece decoration for a gateau or dessert. Store as above.

Run-outs Made in the same way as 'scribbles', but the chocolate outline is filled with a contrasting colour chocolate. This way you end up with solid shapes – good for making numbers, letters of the alphabet, flowers or animals. If you outline in a dark chocolate, fill with white or milk chocolate. Pipe the outline of your design on a chopping board lined with baking parchment. Allow it to set completely, then pipe the contrasting melted chocolate in the gaps and tap the board gently to fill the outline completely and smooth the top. Allow to set firm before carefully peeling from the paper. Store as above.

Chocolate leaves

The safest leaves to use for this are bay leaves, as you'll know for sure that they are not poisonous. Wash the leaves carefully and pat thoroughly dry. Melt the chocolate (see page 32). Using a small pastry brush, coat the leaves with melted chocolate. Place on a chopping board lined with baking parchment and allow to set. Peel away the leaves. Place on a plate, line with baking parchment and chill until required.

Chocolate drops

Melt chocolate (see page 32). Drop small teaspoonfuls of the chocolate in pools onto baking trays lined with baking parchment. Once they are all done, tap the tray lightly on the work surface to smooth out the chocolate. Sprinkle with edible silver dragees, sugar strands or other similar cake decorations and allow to set in a cool place. Once set, peel from the paper. They make tempting 'buttons' to decorate iced cakes and buns. Store as above.

Chocolate cut-outs

Melt chocolate (see page 32) and spread in a thin layer on to a tray or chopping board lined with baking parchment. Leave in a cool place until firm, but not hard (do not refrigerate). Using a sharp knife or small pastry cutters, cut out shapes to your chosen design, and carefully peel away from the paper. Store as above. These cut-outs are great for sticking into whipped cream on top of cakes, trifles, sundaes and other chilled desserts, or laid flat to decorate small iced cakes and muffins.

Chocolate ribbons

Cut out strips of baking parchment about 2.5 x 30cm (1 x 12in). Line up a row of spoons on your work surface (all will become clear!) Brush each parchment strip with melted chocolate and then drape over the handles of the spoons to make waves. Leave until set, then carefully peel away the paper. Break into different lengths as desired and pile on top of cakes and desserts. Dust with cocoa powder or icing sugar if liked. Store as above.

Chocolate cases

You can use chocolate in several ways to encase other ingredients or provide a container for various fillings:

Boxes Melt chocolate (see page 32) and spread in a thin layer on to a tray or chopping board lined with baking parchment. Leave in a cool place until firm, but not hard (do not refrigerate). Using a sharp knife, cut out even sized squares, and peel away from the paper. Place on a plate, line with baking parchment and chill until required. Use to form chocolate edges for cubes of chocolate cake, securing on the sides of the cake using jam or buttercream.

Cups Decide on the size you want to make and either put two cupcake cases or two petit four cases inside each other. Melt chocolate (see page 32), and, using a spoon or pastry brush, completely coat the bottom and inside of the case. Allow to set, then repeat with a second layer of chocolate. Allow to set for at least 2 hours. Carefully peel away the paper case and place the chocolate cup on a flat plate. Cover lightly and keep in the fridge until required. Fill smaller cases with a piped mousse, truffle filling or flavoured whipped cream. Use larger cases as a basket for fruit salad or ice cream.

NOTE: this method would also work well if you wanted to make your own 'free-form' cases using double layers of aluminium foil.

Casing You can make thick bands of chocolate to wrap around circular, freestanding chilled desserts to give them a stunning finish. Simply melt chocolate (see page 32) and then coat on to double-thickness strips of baking parchment. Cut the parchment to fit the size of your chosen dessert. Carefully wrap the wet chocolate strips around the dessert, chocolate-side inwards, working quickly as the chocolate will set on contact. Either chill or freeze depending on the recipe. Carefully peel away the paper, leaving the chocolate in place when ready to serve. This idea works well to give a chocolate 'collar' to set mousses and iced soufflés.

Dipping and coating fruits and sweets

This is one of the simplest and most effective ways of using chocolate as a coating agent. All sorts of sweets, as well as fresh or dried fruit pieces, can be coated in chocolate. Tempered couverture chocolate (see page 27) will give the best result, but any other type of melted chocolate can be used if the dipped item is then chilled immediately. Not all fresh fruit is suitable for chocolate coating – choose either small whole fruits like cherries or kumquats, or if the fruit is cut, make sure the surface is as dry as possible, otherwise the juices from the fruit will spoil the chocolate as it is dipped.

Full coating Use a fondue fork, skewer or specialist dipping fork to lower the sweet or piece of fruit into the chocolate. Turn, to coat completely, and then lift out of the melted chocolate, tapping gently on the edge of the bowl to remove excess chocolate. Place the fruit or sweet on a baking parchment-lined board. If you want to set a decoration on the top or sprinkle with sugar strands, chopped nuts or shredded coconut, it is best to do this as soon as possible before the chocolate sets.

Half dipping Either hold the sweet or fruit between your fingers or a small pair of tongs; half dip the item in melted chocolate and place on baking parchment as above.

NOTE: if using fresh whole or cut fruit, keep in the fridge until ready to serve. It is best served as soon as possible before the fruit deteriorates.

Cocoa stencils

If you're lacking inspiration for a way to finish off the top of a cake, dessert or pie, this decoration is particularly good – especially if you haven't got the time to make an icing, or you want to avoid too much sweetness and yet still add good chocolate flavour. Lay a paper doily on top of the cake, dust lightly with cocoa powder and then carefully remove the doily to reveal the patterned surface. You could add a sprinkling of icing sugar as well, either before or after the cocoa, to add some highlights and a touch of sweetness. You can use any sort of paper template you want: you could even make your own from baking parchment.

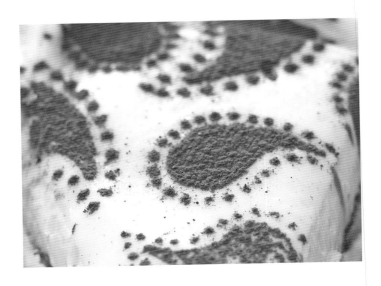

Flavouring and colouring chocolate

Ideally, additional flavourings to complement chocolate should be added to the other ingredients in your chosen recipe. If you are adding liquid flavourings to melting chocolate they have to be added very carefully to prevent burning or causing the chocolate to thicken and become lumpy (see page 33). Drier flavourings like spices, citrus zest or vanilla bean paste can be mixed into melted chocolate, but the chocolate should then be used as quickly as possible.

White chocolate can be coloured using standard food colourings, but remember that the colour achieved will not be true because the basic colour of the chocolate is not pure white. It is best to experiment with a small amount of melted chocolate and a few drops of colouring to make sure you are happy with the shade and to avoid disappointment and wastage. You can use the coloured chocolate to make shells for fillings for homemade chocolates, Easter eggs or for making any of the decorations mentioned in the previous pages.

Tempering

This is the process of gently heating and cooling chocolate to stabilize the emulsification of cocoa solids and butterfat. It is a professional technique carried out using couverture chocolate (see page 27) and allows chocolate to shrink quickly (important for unmoulding) and enables chocolate to be stored at room temperature for longer without loss of texture, flavour or glossy appearance. The professional chocolate-maker would use a special tempering machine, but the technique can be carried out in the domestic kitchen on a small scale.

Melt the couverture chocolate (see page 33), to a temperature of about 45°C (110°F) and stir using a plastic spatula (avoid metal) until completely smooth.

Pour three-quarters of the chocolate on to a clean marble slab or board and spread across the board using the spatula. Scrape the chocolate back into a pool and then spread out again. Continue this process for about 5 minutes until the chocolate is smooth and doesn't form streaks.

Scrape this chocolate back into the bowl with the remaining quarter and mix the two batches together. The tempering process is complete and the chocolate is now ready to use.

Cakes and muffins

No tea-shop trolley or cake-shop counter would be complete without a chocolate cake of some description. Chocolate cakes are a favourite with young and old alike, and are always considered a treat.

In this chapter you'll find chocolate cakes of all different shapes and sizes, and flavours to suit all tastes. I love baking but it still amazes me just how many ways there are to make a chocolate cake, and the different results each method gives. I've tried to include as many as I can. Over the next few pages, you'll find little cupcake and muffins that the kids will love; a classic tea-time loaf cake and also a variety of larger cakes, from white to dark and covering the whole range in between. I've included a gluten-free cake and a light, airy sponge that is low in fat but still has a good chocolatey flavour.

Most of the cakes are covered with frostings and icings and if you've been inspired by what you've read so far, you'll decorate them using the ideas given on pages 34–43.

Chocolate truffle cake

I've baked this for many special occasions and it never fails to impress. For weddings, birthdays or Christmas, it's one of the best ever.

Serves 12

- 450g (15oz) 70% cocoa dark chocolate
- 250g (8oz) unsalted butter
- 6 large eggs, separated
- 250g (8oz) dark brown sugar
- 6 Tbsp dark rum or freshly squeezed orange juice
- 1 tsp vanilla extract
- 180g (6oz) self-raising flour
- 125g (4oz) ground almonds
- 1 quantity Glossy chocolate cream (see page 179)
- Piped chocolate decorations (see page 36)
- Few raspberries, to decorate
- Pouring cream (optional), to serve

Preheat the oven to 180°C/350°F/Gas mark 4. Fill a roasting tin with water in place this in the bottom of the oven as it heats up. Grease and line a 25-cm (10-in) diameter, 5-cm (2-in) deep, round cake tin.

Break the chocolate into pieces and place in a heatproof bowl over a pan of gently simmering water. Cut the butter into small cubes and add to the chocolate. Allow to melt, then remove the bowl from over the water and set aside to cool for 15 minutes.

Meanwhile, in a clean bowl, whisk the egg yolks and sugar together until thick, pale and creamy. In another bowl, whisk the egg whites until stiff but not dry.

Stir the melted chocolate mixture into the whisked egg yolks and sugar. Add the rum or orange juice and vanilla extract. Sieve in the flour and add the ground almonds and whisked egg whites. Carefully fold the ingredients together until well mixed, taking care not to beat too much air out of the mixture. Transfer to the prepared cake tin, smooth the top and bake in the centre of the oven for 50–55 minutes or until just firm to the touch. Allow to cool in the tin on a wire rack for 30 minutes, then remove from the tin and place on the wire rack to cool completely.

To serve, spread the Glossy chocolate cream thickly and evenly over the top and sides of the cake. Decorate, and serve it either on its own or with pouring cream.

Key lime surprise cake

When you think about the mix of eggs and fat used in cake baking it becomes obvious why this recipe uses a shortcut: mayonnaise. Make sure you choose a very plain mayo though – garlic or mustard don't taste nice with chocolate!

Serves 8

- 250g (8oz) self-raising flour
- 60g (2oz) cocoa powder
- ¼ tsp baking powder
- 200g (7oz) light brown sugar
- 1 tsp vanilla extract
- 200ml (7fl oz) cold water
- 225g (7½oz) plain, good-quality mayonnaise

For the topping
- 100g (3½oz) white chocolate
- 30g (1oz) unsalted butter
- 150g (5oz) icing sugar
- Finely grated rind and juice of 1 lime
- Strips of lime zest, to decorate

Preheat the oven to 180°C/350°F/Gas mark 4. Grease and line a 23-cm (9-in) diameter, 5-cm (2-in) deep, round cake tin. Sift the flour, cocoa and baking powder into a mixing bowl and stir in the sugar. Make a well in the centre. Add the vanilla extract, water and mayonnaise, and carefully whisk the ingredients together to form a thick, smooth batter.

Transfer to the prepared cake tin and bake in the oven for 50–60 minutes or until the cake feels firm to the touch. Allow to cool in the tin on a wire rack for 30 minutes, before removing from the tin and placing back on the wire rack until it is completely cool.

Meanwhile, break the chocolate into a small heatproof bowl. Add the butter and place over a saucepan of gently simmering water until melted. Remove the bowl from the water and sieve in the icing sugar. Add the lime rind and mix together, adding sufficient lime juice to form a thick, smooth frosting. Spread over the cooled cake and sprinkle with lime zest to decorate.

Chocolate Swiss roll

This sponge cake takes me back to my school days when this was one of the traditional cake methods I had to perfect to pass my cookery exam. Sifting the flour twice and adding the hot water really makes a difference to the texture.

Serves 6–8

- 3 large eggs
- 100g (3½oz) caster sugar
- 90g (3oz) plain flour
- 2 Tbsp + 1 tsp cocoa powder
- 1 Tbsp hot, boiled water
- 1 quantity Chocolate buttercream (see page 178)
- 100g (3½oz) good-quality cherry conserve or jelly
- 1 Tbsp icing sugar

Preheat the oven to 220°C/425°F/Gas mark 7. Grease a 33 x 23-cm (13 x 9-in) Swiss roll tin. Cut a piece of baking parchment about 5cm (2in) larger all round than the tin. Press the parchment into the tin, creasing to fit the sides. Cut the parchment at the corners of the tin and overlap the cut paper to fit snugly.

Put the eggs and sugar in a large, clean bowl and stand over a large bowl of hot water. Whisk until thick, pale and creamy – about 5 minutes.

Remove from the bowl of water and continue to whisk for a further 3 minutes. You should be able to leave a trail of a spoon in the mixture when it is whisked sufficiently.

Sift the flour and 2 Tbsp cocoa first on to a sheet of greaseproof paper and then again into the creamy mixture. Add the hot water and carefully fold the mixture together using a metal spoon.

Pour into the prepared tin and tilt the tin backwards and forwards to spread the mixture in an even layer. Bake in the oven for 8–10 minutes until well risen and just firm to the touch.

Meanwhile, place a sheet of greaseproof paper on a clean, damp tea towel. Working quickly, turn out the cooked sponge on to the paper and cut off the crusts. Cover with another sheet of greaseproof paper and roll up the cake from a short side, with the paper inside. Wrap in the tea towel and allow to cool.

To serve, carefully unroll the sponge and discard the paper. Spread with Chocolate buttercream and then the conserve or jelly, and roll up again. Dust with icing sugar and remaining cocoa powder. Slice to serve.

White chocolate celebration cake

My sister-in-law Sarah is a great baker – much to the delight of my brother. She baked this cake for my 40th birthday and it was truly delicious. It makes a great alternative dessert.

Serves 10

- 125g (4oz) white chocolate
- 3 large egg whites
- 225g (7½oz) self-raising flour
- 180g (6oz) caster sugar
- 1 Tbsp baking powder
- 180ml (6fl oz) whole milk
- ¾ tsp vanilla extract
- 90g (3oz) unsalted butter, melted
- 1 quantity Glossy white chocolate cream (see page 179)
- Cocoa stencils (see page 41), to decorate

Preheat the oven to 180°C/350°F/ Gas mark 4. Grease and line a deep 20-cm (8-in) cake tin. Break the chocolate into pieces and place in a heatproof bowl over a pan of gently simmering water. Allow to melt, then remove from the water and set aside. Meanwhile, in a large grease-free bowl, whisk the egg whites until stiff but not dry, then set aside. Sift the flour, sugar and baking powder into another bowl. Make a well in the centre and pour in the milk and add the vanilla extract and melted butter. Whisk gently to form a thick batter, then stir in the melted chocolate. Finally fold in the egg whites and pour into the prepared tin. Smooth the top and bake in the oven for about 50 minutes until golden, risen and firm to the touch. Allow to cool in the tin on a wire rack for 10 minutes before removing from the tin and placing back on to the wire rack to cool completely.

When the cake is cool, slice it horizontally in two and spread half of the Glossy white chocolate cream thickly over one half of the cake. Sandwich the cake together and spread the remaining cream thickly over the top. Decorate with a cocoa stencil before serving.

Chocolate orange polenta cake

It can be difficult baking something that's indulgent and decadent if you're on a gluten-free or dairy-free diet, but this should make the grade. It's lovely to serve as a rich dessert.

Serves 8

- 180ml (6fl oz) sunflower oil
- 180g (6oz) light brown sugar
- 2 large eggs
- 2 Tbsp cocoa powder
- 150g (5oz) ground almonds
- Finely grated zest and juice of 1 medium orange
- 90g (3oz) polenta
- ½ tsp baking powder
- ¼ quantity Chocolate sugar syrup (see page 174)
- Fresh orange segments
- Greek yogurt or soya cream, to serve

Preheat the oven to 180°C/350°F/Gas mark 4. Grease and line the base and sides of an 18-cm (7-in) square spring-release cake tin using baking parchment.

Whisk together the sunflower oil with the sugar and eggs. Sieve in the cocoa powder and add the ground almonds, orange zest, polenta and baking powder. Mix together well and pour into the prepared tin and bake for 50–55 minutes until firm to the touch and a skewer inserted into the centre comes out clean.

While the cake is baking, prepare the Chocolate sugar syrup. Stir the orange juice into the warm syrup, then set aside.

Once the cake comes out of the oven, skewer all over with a toothpick and pour the syrup over the warm cake. Cool in the tin on a wire rack, then release from the tin. To serve, arrange the orange segments on top of the cake, with Greek yogurt or soya cream on the side.

Four-layer chiffon cake

An American baking sensation, made with oil instead of butter which gives the sponge a silky-soft texture; hence the name.

Serves 12

- 90g (3oz) 70% cocoa dark chocolate
- 250g (8oz) self-raising flour
- 1 Tbsp baking powder
- 300g (10oz) caster sugar
- 6 eggs, separated
- 100ml (3½fl oz) corn oil
- 100ml (3½fl oz) cold water
- ½ tsp cream of tartar
- 2 quantities of Glossy milk chocolate cream (see page 179)
- 30g (1oz) 70% cocoa dark chocolate, melted (see page 32), for piping

Preheat the oven to 180°C/350°F/Gas mark 4. Grease and line two 23-cm (9-in) round spring-release cake tins with baking parchment. Break the chocolate into pieces and place in a small heatproof bowl over a pan of gently simmering water. Allow to melt, then remove from the water and set aside for 5 minutes.

Meanwhile, sieve the flour and baking powder into a bowl and stir in the sugar. In a separate bowl, mix together the egg yolks, oil and water. In a third bowl, whisk the egg whites with the cream of tartar until stiff.

Make a well in the flour and baking powder, pour the egg and oil mixture into the well and add the warm chocolate. Mix together to form a smooth batter. Carefully fold the egg whites into the chocolate batter until thoroughly mixed. Divide between the two cake tins and bake for about 35 minutes until risen and firm to the touch. Cool for 10 minutes in the tins and then turn on to wire racks to cool completely.

When they have cooled, carefully cut each cake horizontally in half. Spread half of the Glossy milk chocolate cream over three of the layers. Sandwich the layers together in a neat stack and top with the fourth cake layer. Spread the remaining chocolate cream over the top and sides of the cake. Pipe the melted dark chocolate over the top of the cake to decorate – for example, pipe the word 'chocolate' repeatedly over the surface.

Old-fashioned marbled loaf

I love a 'proper' cakey cake – uniced, with a dense, crumbly texture that is ideally accompanied by a cup of tea. If you want to jazz it up a bit, drizzle with some Chocolate glacé icing (see page 179).

Serves 8

- 45g (1½oz) plain chocolate
- 2 tsp hot, boiled water
- ½ tsp vanilla extract
- 180g (6oz) unsalted butter, softened
- 180g (6oz) caster sugar
- 3 large eggs, beaten
- 250g (8oz) plain flour
- 1½ tsp baking powder
- 45g (1½oz) ground almonds
- 1½ Tbsp milk

Preheat the oven to 180°C/350°F/Gas mark 4. Grease and line a 1-kg (2-lb) loaf tin with baking parchment. Break the chocolate into pieces and place in a small heatproof bowl over a pan of gently simmering water. Allow to melt, then remove from the water and set aside to cool for 15 minutes. Stir in the water and vanilla extract.

Put the butter and sugar in a separate bowl and beat together until pale and fluffy. Beat in the eggs one at a time. Sieve in the flour and baking powder and add the ground almonds and milk. Gently fold the dry ingredients into the creamed mixture. Spoon half the mixture into another bowl and mix in the melted chocolate.

Drop alternate spoonfuls of the two mixtures into the prepared tin, gently swirling the two together to give a marbled effect. The mixture should be of dropping consistency; thin with a little more milk if it is too thick. Smooth the top and bake in the oven for about 45 minutes until risen, firm to the touch and a skewer inserted into the centre comes out clean. Cool in the tin for 15 minutes, then turn on to a wire rack to cool completely.

Wrap the cooled cake well and store for 24 hours before serving, thickly sliced.

Chocolate angel cake

This is one of the best fatless sponge cakes I've ever made. It rises well and has a soft, aerated texture. The white frosting is the perfect contrast to a light chocolate sponge interior.

Serves 8–10

- 100g (3½oz) plain flour
- 2 Tbsp cocoa powder
- 180g (6oz) caster sugar
- Pinch of salt
- 7 large egg whites
- 1 level tsp cream of tartar
- 1 tsp vanilla extract
- 1 quantity of White vanilla frosting (see page 177)
- Edible silver dragees, to decorate

Preheat the oven to 180°C/350°F/Gas mark 4. Grease and line a deep 20-cm (8-in) diameter round cake tin with baking parchment. Sift the flour and cocoa powder with 7 Tbsp of the caster sugar and the salt in a bowl. Set aside.

Place the egg whites in a large grease-free bowl and whisk until foamy but not stiff. Add the cream of tartar and 2 Tbsp of the remaining caster sugar. Whisk until the egg whites form soft peaks. Add the vanilla extract and remaining sugar, and fold in using a large metal spoon. Gently sieve in the flour, cocoa and sugar mixture, folding it in as you go.

Transfer the mixture to the prepared tin and smooth the top. Bake in the centre of the oven for 30–35 minutes until firm to the touch and a skewer inserted into the centre comes out clean. Leave to cool in the tin for 15 minutes, then remove from the tin and transfer to a wire rack to cool completely.

Peel away the parchment and slice the cake horizontally in half. Spread half of the White vanilla frosting over one cake half and sandwich the other half on top. Transfer to a serving plate, cover the top with the remaining frosting and leave for 30 minutes to set before serving decorated with silver dragees.

Devil's food cake

I've eaten many versions of this well-known cake – some with fresh chocolate cream and others, like this one, with a thick butter frosting. All the recipes, though, are very chocolatey!

Serves 10

- 125g (4oz) 70% cocoa dark chocolate
- 250g (8oz) self-raising flour
- 275g (9oz) caster sugar
- 300ml (10fl oz) buttermilk
- 125g (4oz) unsalted butter, softened
- 3 eggs, beaten
- 1½ tsp bicarbonate of soda
- ½ tsp baking powder
- 1 tsp vanilla extract
- 1 quantity Dark chocolate fudge frosting (see page 177)
- Dark chocolate curls (see page 35), to decorate

Preheat the oven to 180°C/350°F/Gas mark 4. Grease and line two 23-cm (9-in) round spring-release cake tins with baking parchment. Break the chocolate into pieces and place in a small heatproof bowl over a pan of gently simmering water. Allow to melt, then remove from the water and set aside to cool for 5 minutes.

Put all the remaining ingredients, except the frosting and chocolate curls in a large bowl, and add the warm melted chocolate. Mix all the ingredients together well and then beat for 2 minutes until smooth and creamy.

Divide the mixture between the tins and smooth over the tops. Bake for 35–40 minutes until risen and firm to the touch. Cool in the tins for 10 minutes and then turn on to wire racks to cool completely.

To serve, sandwich the two cake halves together with one third of the Dark chocolate fudge frosting and spread the remaining frosting over the sides and top of the cake. Serve piled high with Chocolate curls.

Pineapple chocolate muffins

Crushed pineapple in a mixture always make it dense and moist. The flavour and texture of these improve with time, so store them, uniced, for at least 24 hours before serving.

Makes 10

- 225g (7½oz) plain flour
- 2 Tbsp cocoa powder
- 1 tsp baking powder
- 1 tsp bicarbonate of soda
- ¼ tsp salt
- 180g (6oz) dark brown sugar
- 180g (6oz) unsalted butter
- 2 eggs, beaten
- 100ml (3½fl oz) whole milk
- 250g (8oz) crushed canned pineapple, drained
- 180g (6oz) icing sugar
- 30g (1oz) unsweetened desiccated coconut
- Dried pineapple slices, to decorate

Preheat the oven to 180°C/350°F/Gas mark 4. Line 10 cups of a deep 12-bun muffin tray with paper muffin cases. Sift the flour, cocoa, baking powder, bicarbonate of soda and salt into a mixing bowl. Stir in the sugar and make a well in the centre.

Melt half the butter and pour into the well along with the eggs and milk to form a thick batter. Fold in the crushed pineapple.

Divide the mixture equally between the muffin cases and bake in the oven for about 30 minutes until risen and lightly golden. Transfer to a wire rack to cool completely. Wrap well and store for 24 hours before serving.

To serve, beat the remaining butter until soft and gradually sieve in the icing sugar, beating well, and add the coconut to form a fluffy icing. Spread thickly over each muffin before serving and top each muffin with a slice of dried pineapple.

Cappuccino muffins

Coffee is one of my favourite flavours and these cakes have a good proportion of coffee and chocolate. You could make mini versions to serve as petit fours.

Makes 12

- 60g (2oz) plain-chocolate covered coffee beans
- 350g (12oz) self-raising flour
- 125g (4oz) light brown sugar
- 200g (7oz) plain chocolate chips
- 2 eggs, beaten
- 125g (4oz) butter, melted
- 200ml (7fl oz) whole milk
- 1 Tbsp icing sugar
- 1 tsp drinking chocolate

Preheat the oven to 190°C/375°F/Gas mark 5. Line a 12-bun muffin tray with 12 paper cases. Grind the chocolate coffee beans in a coffee grinder or blender until fine and well ground.

Sieve the flour into a bowl and fold in the ground coffee beans, sugar and chocolate chips. Make a well in the centre.

Mix the eggs, melted butter and milk together and pour into the well. Mix to form a smooth batter, taking care not to overmix. Divide the batter equally between the paper cases and bake for about 30 minutes until risen and firm to the touch. Transfer to a wire rack to cool.

Serve warm, dusted lightly first with some icing sugar and then a little drinking chocolate.

White chocolate and lemon muffins

This is a reduced fat recipe that produces a surprisingly light muffin. They will keep for a couple of days in an airtight container but are best served warm.

Makes 8

- 250g (8oz) self-raising flour
- ½ tsp baking powder
- 60g (2oz) caster sugar
- 125g (4oz) white chocolate, cut into small chunks
- 2 large eggs, separated
- Finely grated rind and juice of 1 small lemon
- 6 Tbsp low-fat natural yogurt
- 4 Tbsp corn oil
- 4 Tbsp water
- Warmed lemon curd or lemon jelly (optional), to serve

Preheat the oven to 200°C/400°F/Gas mark 6. Line 8 cups of a muffin tray with paper muffin cases. Sieve the flour and baking powder into a bowl and stir in the sugar and chocolate chunks. Make a well in the centre.

Mix together the egg yolks, lemon rind and juice, yogurt, oil and water. Whisk the egg whites in a grease-free bowl until stiff but not too dry. Pour the lemon and yogurt mixture into the well and mix to form a dropping consistency, taking care not to overmix. Gently fold in the egg whites and divide the mixture equally between the muffin cases.

Bake in the oven for about 25 minutes until well risen and golden brown. Transfer to a wire rack to cool. Serve warm, with lemon curd or lemon jelly to spoon over if liked.

Blueberry choc cupcakes

These sweet little cakes would make an ideal treat at a children's party. Lilac-coloured icing gives a pretty finishing touch, but chocolate would be just as good.

Makes 16

- 60g (2oz) cocoa powder
- 200ml (7fl oz) warm, boiled water
- 125g (4oz) butter, softened
- 300g (10oz) light brown sugar
- 2 eggs, beaten
- 180g (6oz) self-raising flour
- 200g (7oz) blueberries, thawed if frozen
- 200g (7oz) icing sugar
- 5–6 tsp unsweetened blueberry juice drink
- Crystallized violets, to decorate

Preheat the oven to 190°C/375°F/Gas mark 5. Put 16 paper cake cases into a tray of bun tins. Sieve the cocoa into a small bowl and whisk in the water.

In another bowl, beat the butter and sugar together until pale and creamy, and gradually beat in the eggs and cocoa mixture. Sieve in the flour and fold the ingredients together, along with the blueberries.

Divide the mixture equally between the cake cases and bake in the oven for about 20 minutes until risen to the tops of the cases and just firm to the touch. Transfer to a wire rack to cool.

For the icing, sift the icing sugar into a bowl and bind together with sufficient blueberry juice to form a smooth, spreadable icing. Spread neatly over each cupcake and decorate with crystallized violets. Allow the icing to set for a few minutes before serving.

Choc chunk and raspberry muffins

Chocolate and raspberry go so well together, the sweetness of the chocolate cutting through the tartness of the raspberry. These muffins are a real treat.

Makes 10

- 250g (8oz) self-raising flour
- 125g (4oz) unbleached caster sugar
- 125g (4oz) milk chocolate chunks
- 2 eggs, beaten
- 150ml (5fl oz) whole milk
- 125g (4oz) butter, melted
- 200g (7oz) fresh raspberries
- 1 quantity Chocolate glacé icing (see page 179, optional)

Preheat the oven to 190°C/375°F/Gas mark 5.
Put 10 paper muffin cases into a tray of deep muffin tins.

Sift the flour into a bowl and gently stir in the sugar and chocolate chunks and make a well in the centre. Mix the eggs, milk and melted butter together and pour into the well, stirring to form a stiff batter, but taking care not to overmix. Carefully fold in the raspberries.

Divide the batter equally between the muffin cases. Smooth the tops slightly and bake in the oven for 35–40 minutes, until risen and lightly golden. Transfer to a wire rack to cool.

Best served warm on day of baking. If you like, they could be topped with Chocolate glacé icing.

Toffee chocolate cupcakes

My favourite chocolates are those with caramel, fudge or toffee centres, and with this in mind, I developed this recipe. I'm sure it will be popular with children and adults alike.

Makes 14

- 200g (7oz) self-raising flour
- 100g (3½oz) unbleached caster sugar
- 2 Tbsp cocoa powder
- 75ml (2½fl oz) sunflower oil
- 75ml (2½fl oz) buttermilk
- 2 eggs, beaten
- 1 Tbsp golden syrup
- 100g (3½oz) toffee-flavoured spread
- 60g (2oz) milk chocolate

Preheat the oven to 160°C/325°F/Gas mark 3. Put 14 paper cupcake cases into a tray of bun tins. Sieve the flour, sugar, cocoa, bicarbonate of soda and baking powder into a bowl and make a well in the centre.

Whisk together the oil, buttermilk, eggs and syrup and pour into the well. Mix together to form a smooth batter, taking care not to overmix. Divide the mixture equally between the cupcake cases and bake in the oven for about 20 minutes until risen and firm to the touch. Transfer to a wire rack to cool.

Slice off the top of each cake and spread with toffee spread. Replace the tops. Break the chocolate into a small heatproof bowl and place over a saucepan of gently simmering water until melted. Drizzle the chocolate over the top of each cupcake. Allow to set for a few minutes before serving.

Pies, tarts and pastries

After cake-baking, pastry-making is next on my list of favourites. I prefer the flavour and texture of homemade pastry – it's usually more crumbly, buttery and flavoursome. But it does take time and a bit of skill, and if you haven't got the confidence, then there are some good ready-made pastry doughs and cases available. Choose a good-quality brand so that the flavour of the pastry doesn't detract from the filling or topping that you're making to go with it.

When I was researching recipes for this chapter, I soon discovered that there aren't that many classic chocolate pies. What you'll find over the next few pages are a collection of favourites with a chocolate addition, such as the nutty and sweet Chocolate pecan pie, some classic pastries like the French breakfast-time treat Mini pain au chocolat, alongside some new ideas – Chocolate date strudel with crisp, buttery flakes of pastry, and a creamy White chocolate and berry pie.

Although pies are usually made from short pastry, I've included recipes using filo, choux and puff pastry as well as pie cases made using cookie crumbs. I hope you enjoy them as much I as did!

Chocolate and cherry puffs

These pastries are straightforward to assemble and they can be prepared in advance. Simply bake just before serving and serve while the chocolate is still molten.

Makes 8

- 500g (1lb) ready-made puff pastry, thawed if frozen
- 180g (6oz) plain chocolate
- 8 Tbsp cherry pie filling
- 1 egg, beaten

Preheat the oven to 200°C/400°F/Gas mark 6. On a lightly-floured surface, roll out the pastry to approximately a 40-cm (16-in) square. Cut out sixteen 10-cm (4-in) diameter circles using a pastry cutter.

Arrange eight circles on a large baking sheet lined with baking parchment. Divide the chocolate into eight pieces and place chocolate in the centre of each circle. Top each piece of pastry with 1 Tbsp cherry pie filling. Brush the edges with beaten egg and cover with the remaining pastry circles. Seal the edges well.

Slash the tops lightly with a sharp knife and brush with beaten egg. Bake for 20–25 minutes until puffed up and golden. Best served warm.

Rich chocolate and apricot tart

If your taste in chocolate veers towards the bitter end of the scale, then this tart is perfect for you. You can make it with plain or an unsweetened, lesser cocoa percentage chocolate if you prefer.

Serves 8

- 1 quantity Chocolate pastry (see page 176) or 1 ready-made 23-cm (9-in) chocolate pie crust
- 6 Tbsp good quality apricot conserve or jelly, softened
- 125g (4oz) unsalted butter
- 150g (5oz) unsweetened or 85% (or above) cocoa dark chocolate, broken into pieces
- 3 eggs
- 90g (3oz) caster sugar
- Cocoa powder and icing sugar, to dust
- Crème fraiche, to serve

Preheat the oven to 200°C/400°F/Gas mark 6. Make and bake the Chocolate pastry case. Reduce the oven temperature to 180°C/350°F/Gas mark 4.

Spread the apricot conserve in a thin layer over the base of the pastry case. Put the butter and chocolate in a heatproof bowl over a saucepan of gently simmering water until melted. Remove from the water and set aside. Meanwhile, whisk the eggs and sugar together until pale and creamy.

Gently fold the melted chocolate and butter into the egg mixture until evenly incorporated and spoon over the pastry. Smooth the surface and bake for about 25 minutes until the top has formed a crust. Stand for 10 minutes before removing from the tin if you plan to serve it hot, otherwise allow to cool in the tin and then chill for at least 1 hour before serving. Serve hot or cold, dusted with cocoa and icing sugar, accompanied by crème fraîche.

Mini pain au chocolat

Half pastry, half bread – it's deliciously flaky with a soft chocolate centre.

Makes 12

- 275g (9oz) plain flour
- 1 Tbsp caster sugar
- ½ tsp salt
- 30g (1oz) lard or white vegetable fat
- 1 tsp fast-acting dried yeast
- 150ml (5fl oz) whole milk, slightly warm
- 90g (3oz) piece unsalted butter
- 1 egg, beaten
- 12 small pieces (approx. 60g/2oz) plain chocolate
- 30g (1oz) icing sugar

Sift the flour into a bowl and stir in the sugar and salt. Rub in the fat to form fine breadcrumbs. Stir in the yeast.

Make a well in the centre and pour in most of the milk. Mix with your fingers, then tip on to a lightly-floured work surface. Bring together and knead lightly until you have a dough slightly softer than a pastry mixture; add more milk if necessary. Lightly flour the bowl and place the dough back in it. Cover loosely and stand in a warm place for about an hour until doubled in size.

Gently reknead the dough to form a smooth ball. Roll the dough out to an oblong 38 x 15cm (15 x 6in) and place the piece of butter in the centre. Fold the dough over the butter, top and bottom, to cover it and press the edges to seal. Roll the dough out gently to form an oblong the same size as before. Fold the top third down and the bottom third up, and turn 90 degrees. Cover and rest for 10 minutes. Repeat the rolling, folding and turning twice more. Transfer to a floured plate, cover and chill for 30 minutes.

Roll out to 30 x 20cm (12 x 8in). Cut in two lengthways and then cut each piece into six oblongs to give 12 pieces. Brush with beaten egg and then place a piece of chocolate in the centre. On each piece fold the bottom third up and the top third down. Turn over and press down to seal the edges and enclose the chocolate.

Transfer to a large baking sheet and cover loosely with greased clear food wrap. Stand in a warm place for about 30 minutes until slightly risen. Preheat the oven to 220°C/425°F/Gas mark 7.

Brush with beaten egg again and bake for about 15 minutes until puffed up and golden. Transfer to a wire rack to cool. Best served warm, dusted with icing sugar.

Tiramisu chocolate choux buns

Choux is a light puffy pastry, the perfect casing for a creamy or custard filling. So that the pastry stays crisp, only fill just before serving.

Serves 8

For the choux pastry
- 150g (5oz) plain flour
- 2 Tbsp cocoa powder
- ½ tsp salt
- 1 Tbsp caster sugar
- 250ml (8fl oz) cold water
- 125g (4oz) unsalted butter, cut into pieces
- Approx. 4 eggs, beaten

For the filling
- 150ml (5fl oz) whipping cream
- 2 Tbsp icing sugar
- 150g (5oz) mascarpone cheese
- 1 tsp instant coffee granules, dissolved in 2 tsp cooled boiled water
- 1 Tbsp brandy (optional)

To serve
- 1 quantity Chocolate glacé icing (see page 179)
- Cocoa powder, to dust

Preheat the oven to 220°C/425°F/Gas mark 7. Lightly grease a large baking sheet. Sift the flour, cocoa, salt and sugar on to a sheet of greaseproof paper. Put the water in a saucepan with the butter and bring to the boil.

Remove from the heat and add all the sieved ingredients immediately. Beat vigorously until the mixture forms a smooth ball in the saucepan. Cool for 10 minutes, then gradually beat in sufficient egg to form a thick, shiny mixture that gently drops off the spoon.

Sprinkle the baking sheet lightly with water and then drop eight mounds approximately 7.5cm (3in) diameter, at least 5cm (2in) apart on the baking sheet. Bake for 40 minutes, until puffed up and firm. Using a serrated knife, slice one quarter of the way round the side of each bun to allow the steam to escape. Arrange on a wire rack to cool completely.

For the filling, whip the cream until just peaking. Sieve in the icing sugar and add the mascarpone cheese, coffee and brandy, if using, and continue whisking until the mixture is firm enough to spoon. Cover and chill until required.

When ready to serve, spoon the coffee cream filling into the centre of each bun and carefully spread with Chocolate glacé icing. Serve dusted with cocoa powder.

Chocolate pecan pie

A classic favourite with a chocolate twist. It's a great way to enjoy the sweet earthiness of pecan nuts.

Serves 8

- 1 quantity Chocolate pastry (see page 176) or 300g (10oz) ready-made sweet shortcrust pastry
- 90g (3oz) plain chocolate
- 30g (1oz) unsalted butter
- 60g (2oz) caster sugar
- 1½ tsp cornflour
- Pinch salt
- 150ml (5fl oz) maple syrup
- 2 eggs, beaten
- 200g (7oz) pecan nuts
- Vanilla ice cream, to serve

Preheat the oven to 180°C/350°F/Gas mark 4. Make the Chocolate pastry and roll out and line a 23-cm (9-in) loose-bottomed flan tin. Chill until required.

Break the chocolate into pieces and place in a small heatproof bowl. Add the butter and stand the bowl over a pan of gently simmering water. Allow to melt, then remove from the water and set aside to cool for 15 minutes.

Meanwhile, make the filling. In a mixing bowl, whisk together the remaining ingredients, except the pecan nuts, and then whisk in the melted chocolate and butter. Transfer to a jug.

Arrange the pecan nuts neatly in the pastry case and stand on a baking sheet. Pour over the filling and bake in the oven for about 50 minutes until set. Leave to cool in the tin, then transfer to a serving plate. Best served with vanilla ice cream.

Chocolate almond and pear tart

Chocolate and pears go together almost as well as strawberries and cream. This tart is just as good hot or cold – I prefer it just warm though, so that the almond flavour comes through.

Serves 6–8

- 1 quantity Chocolate pastry (see page 176) or 300g (10oz) ready-made sweet shortcrust pastry
- 125g (4oz) unsalted butter, softened
- 125g (4oz) caster sugar
- 2 eggs
- 125g (4oz) ground almonds
- 2 Tbsp cocoa powder
- ½ tsp almond extract
- 410-g (14-oz) can pear halves in natural juice, drained
- 15g (½oz) flaked almonds
- 1 Tbsp icing sugar, to dust
- Pouring cream, to serve

Preheat the oven to 190°C/375°F/Gas mark 5. Make the Chocolate pastry and roll out and line a 23-cm (9-in) loose-bottomed flan tin. Chill until required.

In a mixing bowl, cream together the butter and sugar until pale and creamy. Gradually beat in the eggs and ground almonds. Sieve in the cocoa powder and fold in along with the almond extract. Spoon the mixture into the pastry case and smooth the top.

Cut the pear halves in half and pat dry with kitchen paper. Gently press the pear slices into the almond filling. Sprinkle with flaked almonds and bake in the oven for 35–40 minutes until the almonds are lightly golden and the sponge is firm to the touch. Stand for 10 minutes before removing from the tin. Dust with icing sugar and serve hot or cold with pouring cream.

Chocolate banoffee pie

This name comes from the combination of banana and toffee in the filling. I've added some chocolate into the mix and piled it high with whipped cream, making it an even more indulgent dessert.

Serves 6

- 90g (3oz) butter
- 250g (8oz) double chocolate chip cookies, crushed
- 3 ripe medium-sized bananas
- 397-g (14-oz) can condensed milk
- 1 Tbsp cocoa powder
- 300ml (10fl oz) double cream
- Grated milk chocolate, to decorate

Try not to brown the condensed milk too much otherwise the filling will set too hard.

Grease the bases and sides of six individual 8-cm (3-in) loose-bottomed cake tins or cake rings. Melt the butter in a saucepan, then remove from the heat. Mix the crushed cookies with the melted butter and divide between the six tins. Press firmly into the base of each. Slice the bananas thinly and arrange over the biscuit base. Cover and chill until required.

Pour the condensed milk into a saucepan, bring to the boil and simmer over a medium heat, stirring, until the milk turns a toffee colour. Remove from the heat, sieve over the cocoa and add 6 Tbsp double cream and mix well. Spoon the toffee filling over the bananas and biscuit base. Cover and chill for 30 minutes.

When ready to serve, remove the pies from the tins and place on serving plates. Whip the remaining double cream and pile on top of each one. Sprinkle with grated chocolate and serve.

Chocolate date strudel

Fresh dates have a sticky, sweet texture that makes them a perfect filling for a pastry case. Combined with chocolate, nuts and spice, this pastry creation makes a delicious feast on a winter's day.

Serves 8

- 60g (2oz) chocolate cake crumbs
- 30g (1oz) flaked almonds, toasted
- 250g (8oz) fresh dates, pitted and finely chopped
- 125g (4oz) plain chocolate chips
- 1 tsp ground cinnamon
- ½ tsp finely grated orange rind
- 2 Tbsp freshly-squeezed orange juice
- 8 large sheets filo pastry
- 90g (3oz) unsalted butter, melted
- 2 Tbsp icing sugar
- 1 tsp cocoa powder
- Pouring cream, to serve

Preheat the oven to 200°C/400°F/Gas mark 6. Line a large baking sheet with baking parchment. In a bowl, mix together the cake crumbs, almonds, dates, chocolate chips, cinnamon, orange rind and juice and mix well.

Lay four sheets of filo pastry on the work surface, overlapping as necessary, to form a rectangle approximately 50 x 36cm (20 x 14in). Brush well with melted butter to secure together. Layer the remaining pastry on top in the same way, brushing all over with butter.

Spread the date mixture evenly down the centre of the pastry to within 2.5cm (1in) of either end. Fold over the top and bottom pastry edge on top of the filling, buttering to seal. Fold the pastry over from the long sides to completely cover the filling, and brush with butter to seal. Transfer to the prepared baking sheet and brush with the remaining butter.

Bake in the oven for about 40 minutes until crisp and golden. Serve hot, dusted with icing sugar and cocoa and accompanied with pouring cream.

Chocolate treacle tart

A variation on a favourite recipe from my school days. A comforting pudding, but it is also lovely cold, drizzled with orange glacé icing.

Serves 6–8

- 1 quantity Chocolate pastry (see page 176 or 300g (10oz) readymade sweet pastry
- 200g (7oz) golden or corn syrup
- 30g (1oz) treacle or molasses
- 30g (1oz) unsalted butter
- 60g (2oz) 70% cocoa plain chocolate, broken into pieces
- ½ tsp finely grated orange rind
- 2 Tbsp freshly squeezed orange juice
- 90g (3oz) fresh white breadcrumbs

Preheat the oven to 200°C/400°F/Gas mark 6. Roll out three-quarters of the pastry on a lightly floured surface and use to line a 20-cm (8-in) loose-bottomed flan tin. Cover and chill while making the filling.

Put the syrup, treacle, butter and chocolate in a saucepan and heat gently until melted. Remove from the heat and set aside to cool but do not allow to set, then stir in the orange rind and juice.

Sprinkle the breadcrumbs evenly over the base of the pastry case, then slowly pour over the melted chocolate syrup. Roll out the remaining pastry thinly into an oblong 20-cm (8-in) long and cut several thin strips, re-rolling the pastry as necessary. Brush the edge of the tart with water and stick the strips to the pastry case, forming a lattice pattern over the chocolate breadcrumbs.

Transfer to a baking tray and bake for 25–30 minutes until the filling has set and the pastry is firm. Leave to stand for 10 minutes before removing from the tin. Best served warm with pouring cream or custard.

White chocolate and berry pie

The very rich and indulgent white chocolate in this pie is perfectly accompanied by the sharp-sweet flavour of summer berries and currants. Orange segments also make a good accompaniment.

Serves 8–10

- 150g (5oz) butter
- 250g (8oz) shortbread fingers, crushed
- 250g (8oz) white chocolate
- 300ml (10fl oz) sour cream
- 2 Tbsp dark rum (optional)
- 300ml (10fl oz) double cream
- 250g (8oz) prepared, assorted summer berries
- White chocolate decorations, to finish

★ ★ ★ ★ ★ ★ ★ ★ ★ ★ ★ ★

This dessert will also work with milk or continental plain chocolate.

Grease and line the base and sides of a 20-cm (8-in) spring-release cake tin. Melt 90g (3oz) of the butter in a saucepan, remove from the heat and then mix in the crushed shortbread. Press into the base of the tin. Chill until required.

Break the chocolate into pieces and place in a small heatproof bowl. Add the remaining butter and stand the bowl over a pan of gently simmering water. Allow to melt, then remove from the water and stir in the sour cream and rum if using.

Whip the double cream to form soft peaks and fold into the chocolate cream. Spoon over the biscuit base and smooth the top. Chill for at least 6 hours or overnight.

When ready to serve, remove from the tin and place on a serving plate. Top with the berries and finish off with white chocolate decorations of your choice (see pages 34–43 for ideas). Cut into slices to serve.

Chocolate custard tarts

These little custard tarts make a perfect tea-time treat. If you're short on time, use 300g (10oz) ready-made shortcrust pastry instead of making your own.

Makes 12

- 1 quantity Chocolate pastry (see page 176) or 300g (10oz) ready-made shortcrust pastry
- 1 egg yolk
- 2 Tbsp caster sugar
- 1 Tbsp vanilla sugar
- 1 Tbsp plain flour
- 250ml (8fl oz) whole milk
- 1 Tbsp cornflour
- 30g (1oz) unsweetened or 85% (or above) cocoa dark chocolate, grated

Preheat the oven to 200°C/400°F/Gas mark 6. Make the Chocolate pastry and roll out thinly on a lightly-floured surface. Using a 7.5-cm (3-in) diameter round pastry cutter, cut out 12 circles, re-rolling the pastry as necessary, and press into patty tins. Lightly prick the bases and bake in the oven for about 15–20 minutes until set and firm. Set aside.

In a heatproof bowl, whisk the egg yolk and sugars together until pale, thick and creamy. Whisk in the flour with 1 Tbsp milk, then add the cornflour and a further 1 Tbsp milk to make a smooth paste. Pour the remaining milk into a saucepan and add the grated chocolate. Heat gently, stirring, until the chocolate melts, then bring to just below boiling point and then pour over the egg and flour paste, whisking until smooth and well combined. Transfer to a saucepan and stir over a low heat until it comes to the boil and then cook for a further 2 minutes until thick, smooth and glossy.

Remove from the heat and spoon some into each pastry case. Smooth the tops, cover the surface with buttered greaseproof paper and leave to cool completely. Chill until ready to serve.

Brownies, cookies and bakes

This chapter contains two of my all-time personal favourites, so it is probably the section I enjoyed writing and trying out the most. There are so many chocolate bakes to choose from it was difficult to narrow the selection down, but I'm sure you'll like the next few recipes as much as I do.

No chocolate book would be complete without brownies and you'll find two different recipes, as well as a white chocolate version to try. Cookies are also chocolate classics and I've included two recipes – Double chocolate and Cookie sandwiches – both are very moreish and delicious. You'll find a healthier-style tray bake of cereal, dried fruit and chocolate chips, and two recipes for chocolate breads – one French and one Italian.

I've left revealing my two favourites until last. Crisp, sugary meringues are the first, and here I've given them a chocolate twist, and Trillionaire's shortbread – the combination of buttery shortbread, thick caramel and three kinds of chocolate – is really very hard to beat!

Flourless mint choc brownies

These brownies are the perfect treat for anyone on a gluten-free diet. The texture is dense, truffley and very chocolatey, and the peppermint cream topping makes them even more yummy!

Makes 16

- 250g (8oz) 70% cocoa dark chocolate
- 250g (8oz) unsalted butter, cut into small pieces
- 200g (7oz) light brown sugar
- 4 eggs, beaten
- 150g (5oz) ground almonds
- 1½ tsp baking powder
- 60g (2oz) milk chocolate chunks
- 225g (7½oz) chocolate-coated peppermint cream wafers

Preheat the oven to 160°C/325°F/Gas mark 3. Grease and line with baking parchment a deep 23-cm (9-in) square cake tin. Break the chocolate into pieces and place in a heatproof bowl. Add the butter and stand the bowl over a pan of gently simmering water. Allow to melt, then remove from the water and stir in the sugar. Set aside to cool for 10 minutes.

Gradually whisk the eggs into the chocolate to make a thick, glossy mixture. Add the ground almonds, baking powder and chocolate chunks, and carefully fold in until well combined.

Transfer to the prepared tin and smooth over the top. Bake in the oven for about 1 hour, until firm and a skewer inserted into the centre comes out clean. Arrange the peppermint wafers neatly over the top and return to the oven for 2–3 minutes until just melted. Leave to cool completely in the tin, then remove and wrap. Store for 24 hours.

To serve, cut into 16 equal portions. If you can leave them alone, these brownies will keep for about a week in an airtight container.

Blondies

If the familiar dark chocolate tray bake is called a brownie, then it makes sense that a white chocolate version is a blondie. Be warned, they're very moreish!

Makes 16

- 350g (12oz) white chocolate, broken into small pieces
- 90g (3oz) butter
- 4 eggs, beaten
- 150g (5oz) unbleached caster sugar
- 30g (1oz) vanilla sugar
- 180g (6oz) self-raising flour
- 180g (6oz) ground almonds
- 60g (2oz) milk chocolate

Preheat the oven to 180°C/350°F/Gas mark 4. Grease and line with baking parchment an 18 x 28-cm (7 x 11-in) rectangular cake tin. Place 125g (4oz) white chocolate pieces in a heatproof bowl with the butter. Place the bowl over a saucepan of gently simmering water. Allow to melt then remove from the water and cool for 10 minutes.

Beat in the eggs and sugars. Sieve in the flour and add the ground almonds, and carefully fold into the mixture along with 180g (6oz) chocolate pieces until well combined.

Transfer to the prepared tin and smooth over the top. Bake in the oven for about 40 minutes until risen, firm and golden. Allow to cool in the tin, then cut into 16 pieces. Carefully remove from the tin and transfer to a wire rack.

Melt the remaining white chocolate and the milk chocolate separately. Spoon a little of the two chocolates on to each slice and gently mix together, using a skewer, to give a marbled effect. Allow to set before serving.

Double chocolate cookies

Nothing beats a freshly-baked chocolate cookie in the comfort stakes. These soft-bake treats are really easy to make and quick to cook – you'll be asked to make them again and again.

Makes 24

- 180g (6oz) butter, softened
- 150g (5oz) light brown sugar
- 1 egg
- 225g (7½oz) plain flour
- 30g (1oz) cocoa powder
- Pinch of salt
- ½ tsp baking powder
- 150g (5oz) milk chocolate chunks

Preheat the oven to 190°C/375°F/Gas mark 5. In a bowl, cream together the butter and sugar until pale and creamy. Beat in the egg.

Sieve in the flour, cocoa, salt and baking powder. Add the chocolate chunks and mix to form a soft dough.

Drop heaped teaspoonfuls, spaced well apart, on large baking sheets lined with baking parchment. Press down lightly and bake for about 12 minutes until spread and just set. Cool on the sheets for about 10 minutes until beginning to firm up, then transfer to a wire rack. Best served warm.

Chocolate cookie sandwiches

Viennese cookie dough is one of the most buttery you can make, it practically dissolves in your mouth. These cookies will be the talk of any coffee morning or afternoon tea.

Makes 8

- 125g (4oz) butter, softened
- 60g (2oz) + 1 Tbsp icing sugar
- 100g (3½oz) plain flour
- 2 Tbsp cocoa powder
- 30g (1oz) ground almonds
- Few drops vanilla extract
- ½ quantity Chocolate buttercream (see page 178)
- ¼ tsp ground cardamom

Preheat the oven to 180°C/350°F/Gas mark 4. Put the butter in a mixing bowl and sieve over 60g (2oz) icing sugar. Beat until pale and creamy.

Sieve in the flour and cocoa powder, and add the ground almonds and vanilla extract. Mix together to form a firm cookie dough.

Put the dough in a large piping bag fitted with a 1-cm (½-in) star nozzle. Pipe eight stars on each of two large baking sheets lined with baking parchment – the cookies will spread and flatten on baking. Bake in the oven for about 15 minutes until firm. Cool on the sheets for 15 minutes, then transfer onto a wire rack to cool completely.

Make the Chocolate buttercream, adding the ground cardamom to flavour. Thickly spread the buttercream over the unpiped side of eight cookies and sandwich together with an uniced cookie. Serve dusted with remaining icing sugar.

Trillionaire's shortbread

Friends and family know that if this triple-chocolate bake is on the menu, then I have to have some. It amazes me just how many variations I've tried, but this is my favourite. It keeps for about a week in the fridge.

Makes 24

- ½ quantity Chocolate shortbread (see page 184)

For toffee filling
- 250g (8oz) unsalted butter
- 250g (8oz) unbleached caster sugar
- 4 Tbsp golden syrup
- 397g (14-oz) can sweetened condensed milk

For chocolate topping
- 90g (3oz) plain chocolate
- 90g (3oz) milk chocolate
- 90g (3oz) white chocolate

Make up the half quantity of shortbread as directed on page 184, pressing it thinly in the tin. Bake for about 50 minutes and leave in the tin, uncut, to cool.

For the toffee filling, put the butter, sugar, syrup and condensed milk in a saucepan and heat gently, stirring until the sugar dissolves. Raise the heat and bring the mixture to a gentle boil, stirring all the time, and simmer gently for about 5 minutes until the mixture has thickened and is a creamy fudge colour. Pour over the shortbread and allow to cool.

Break the chocolate into three small heatproof bowls and place the bowls over saucepans of gently simmering water. Allow to melt, then remove from the water.

Place alternate teaspoonfuls of the melted chocolate on top of the toffee. Tap the tin on the work surface so that the chocolates merge together, then drag a skewer through the chocolate to create a feathered effect. Tap the tin again to smooth the chocolate and set aside in a cool place until firm. If the chocolate sets too firm (in the fridge) it will be more difficult to cut.

Use a sharp knife to cut the shortbread into 24 equal pieces (it is very rich so don't be tempted to cut fewer, larger pieces!), and carefully lift from the tin. Chill until required, but stand at room temperature for a few minutes before serving.

Chocolate and prune macaroons

Adding prunes to a chocolate mixture enhances the chocolatey flavour and gives a moist, sticky texture to the bake which improves on storing. Use soft prunes and they will practically disappear in the mixture.

Makes 16

- 250g (8oz) pitted no-need-to-soak prunes, finely chopped
- 250ml (8fl oz) cold water
- 60g (2oz) cocoa powder
- 125g (4oz) butter
- 250g (8oz) dark brown sugar
- 2 eggs, beaten
- ½ tsp almond extract
- 180g (6oz) ground almonds
- 1 tsp bicarbonate of soda
- ¼ tsp baking powder
- ½ quantity Dark chocolate fudge frosting (see page 177)

Preheat the oven to 180°C/350°F/Gas mark 4. Grease and line with baking parchment an 18 x 28-cm (7 x 11-in) oblong cake tin. Put the prunes, water, cocoa, butter and sugar in a large saucepan and heat gently until the butter melts, the sugar dissolves and the mixture is dark and treacley. Remove from the heat and cool for 10 minutes.

Stir in the remaining ingredients except the frosting and then pour into the prepared tin. Smooth the top and bake in the oven for about 45 minutes until firm to the touch and a skewer inserted into the centre comes out clean. Allow to cool in the tin, then remove and wrap. Store for 24 hours before serving.

To serve, spread the Dark chocolate fudge frosting over the chocolate bake. Cut into 16 bars.

Fruity chocolate cereal bars

A chewy bar that packs a punch on flavour and has a wholesome texture. These would make a great treat for a lunch box.

Makes 12

- 60g (2oz) sultanas
- 60g (2oz) no-need-to-soak dried apricots, finely chopped
- 180g (6oz) plain flour
- Pinch of salt
- 125g (4oz) porridge oats
- 125g (4oz) milk or plain chocolate chunks
- 100g (3½oz) unsalted butter or margarine
- 100g (3½oz) caster sugar
- 3 Tbsp golden syrup

Preheat the oven to 180°C/350°F/Gas mark 4. Grease and line with baking parchment an 18-cm (7-in) square cake tin. In a mixing bowl, mix together the sultanas, apricots, flour, salt, oats and chocolate chunks.

In a small saucepan, gently melt together the butter, sugar and syrup without boiling. Cool for 10 minutes, then stir into the dry ingredients until well mixed and coated in the melted butter syrup.

Press into the prepared tin and bake in the oven for about 30 minutes until lightly golden. Cut into 12 bars and allow to cool in the tin.

Chocolate meringues

The secret of making a good meringue is patience. You need to keep the oven heat low, and cook the meringues on a low shelf for a long time. This way they 'dry out' rather than cook. These have just a very delicate chocolate flavour.

Makes 4

- 4 egg whites
- 200g (7oz) caster sugar
- 1 tsp vanilla extract
- 4 tsp cocoa powder

For the topping
- 150ml (5fl oz) double cream
- 6 pieces rose-flavoured Turkish delight, finely chopped
- 4 Tbsp good-quality strawberry jam
- Fresh strawberries, to serve
- Fruit sauce made with strawberries (see page 176), to serve

Preheat the oven to 130°C/250°F/Gas mark ½. In a large grease-free bowl, whisk the egg whites until very stiff and dry. Whisk in half the sugar. Fold in the remaining sugar and vanilla extract carefully using a large metal spoon. Sift the cocoa on top and gently marble it through the meringue. Pile four large mounds on to a large baking sheet lined with baking parchment, and smooth off the tops a little using the back of a spoon. Bake on the bottom shelf of the oven for about 2 hours until the meringues are firm and still quite pale – prop the oven door open slightly if they start to over-colour. Switch off the heat and leave to cool in the oven.

When ready to serve, whip the cream until softly peaking and fold in the Turkish delight and strawberry jam to give a rippled effect. Serve the meringues with a dollop of the fruity cream on top, accompanied by fresh strawberries and a little fruit sauce.

★ ★ ★ ★ ★ ★ ★ ★ ★ ★ ★

The plain meringues will keep in an airtight container for several days. Once topped or filled meringues should be eaten as soon as possible – refrigerated meringue will soften and dissolve quite quickly.

Mini orange brioche surprises

A lovely breakfast treat. Serve warm so that when you tear them open they ooze with melted chocolate. Delicious with marmalade for extra zing.

Makes 4

- 250g (8oz) strong white bread flour
- ½ tsp salt
- 1 Tbsp caster sugar
- 1¼ tsp instant or fast-acting dried yeast
- ½ tsp finely grated orange zest
- 30g (1oz) candied orange peel, finely chopped
- 3 Tbsp whole milk, slightly warm
- 2 eggs, beaten
- 60g (2oz) unsalted butter, melted
- 4 pieces (approx. 30g/1oz) plain chocolate
- 1 egg yolk mixed with 1 Tbsp cold water, to glaze

Sieve the flour, salt and caster sugar into a bowl and stir in the dried yeast, orange zest and orange peel. Make a well in the centre.

Mix together the milk and beaten egg with the melted butter and pour into the centre of the well. Mix the ingredients together with your fingers, then tip on to a lightly-floured work surface, bring together and knead lightly for about 5 minutes until you have a dough slightly softer than a pastry mixture. Lightly flour the bowl and place the dough back in it. Cover loosely and stand in a warm place for about an hour until doubled in size.

Gently reknead the dough to form a smooth ball. Cut into four equal portions, flatten and place a piece of chocolate in the centre of each. Bring the dough up around the chocolate and form into a ball. If you have four 10-cm (4-in) individual brioche tins, grease them and place a dough ball in each, otherwise greased muffin tins will work just as well. Cover loosely with lightly-oiled clear food wrap and leave in a warm place for about 45 minutes until doubled in size. Preheat the oven to 200°C/400°F/Gas mark 6.

Glaze the brioche with the beaten egg yolk mixture and bake in the oven for 20–25 minutes until risen and richly golden. Transfer to a wire rack to cool slightly. Serve warm.

Pane al cioccolato

A sweet bread from Italy, this is perfect sliced and served spread with mascarpone or ricotta cheese. If you like nuts, you could also replace the chocolate chips with chopped walnuts.

Serves 12

- 400g (14oz) strong white bread flour
- 30g (1oz) cocoa powder
- ½ tsp salt
- 2 Tbsp dark brown sugar
- 30g (1oz) unsalted butter
- 1 tsp instant or fast-acting dried yeast
- 60g (2oz) plain chocolate chips
- 250ml (8fl oz) whole milk, slightly warm
- 1 egg white, beaten
- 1 Tbsp caster sugar

Sieve the flour, cocoa and salt into a bowl and stir in the brown sugar. Rub in the butter and stir in the yeast and chocolate chips. Make a well in the centre.

Pour the milk into the centre of the well. Mix with your fingers, then tip on to a lightly-floured work surface, bring together and knead lightly for about 5 minutes until you have a firm, pliable dough. Lightly flour the bowl and place the dough back in it. Cover loosely and stand in a warm place for about an hour until doubled in size.

Gently reknead the dough to form a smooth ball. Place in the centre of a lightly-greased baking sheet. Cover loosely with oiled, clear food wrap and leave in a warm place for about 45 minutes or until doubled in size. Preheat the oven to 200°C/400°F/Gas mark 6.

Brush the dough ball all over with egg white and sprinkle with sugar. Bake in the oven for about 30 minutes until risen and firm – it should sound hollow when tapped. Cool for 15 minutes then transfer to a wire rack to cool completely. Serve warm or cold.

Hot puddings

I have to be honest now; I rarely choose a chocolate pudding when it comes to dessert. Not because I don't like them, it's usually because I'm too full and I find the chocolate too rich to enjoy it properly. I prefer to have my chocolate as a meal on its own – very naughty but ever so nice – and that way I can enjoy the chocolate experience to the maximum!

I do have several friends who always have a chocolate pudding, so this chapter's dedicated to them – they know who they are! I've put some real rib-sticking, 'proper', puddings in this chapter, alongside lighter choices, so you should find something to suit every occasion.

For a filling treat why not try the Chocolate and ginger pudding with lashings of chocolate custard, or the thick and creamy Chocolate risotto – both guaranteed to hit the spot on a cold day. The Dark chocolate espresso soufflé is a much lighter option and packed with flavour. If you want to serve something very different to your guests, give them a bowl of Fragrant chocolate soup – it's full of exotic flavours and gives a real chocolate 'hit' after a meal. I'm sure it'll be a real talking point.

Fragrant chocolate soup

Really a variation on a chocolate fondue, this rich, dark recipe has a citrus edge. Best served warm for maximum flavour, but it will thicken as it cools. Serve in small amounts.

Serves 6

- 2 stalks lemongrass
- 1 lime
- 2 star anise
- 4 Tbsp light brown sugar
- 400-ml (14-oz) can coconut milk
- 60g (2oz) unsweetened or 85% (or above) cocoa dark chocolate, grated
- 150ml (5fl oz) double cream
- 60g (2oz) milk chocolate, grated
- Finely shredded lime zest, to decorate

Trim the stalk from the lemongrass, split the bulb in half and place in a saucepan. Using a vegetable peeler, pare off the rind from the lime into the saucepan. Extract the juice and set aside.

Add the star anise and sugar to the saucepan and stir in the coconut milk. Slowly bring to the boil, then turn off the heat, cover and allow to infuse for 30 minutes. Stir in the lime juice, pour through a strainer and set aside.

When ready to serve, put the unsweetened chocolate in a saucepan with the cream. Heat very gently to melt the chocolate and mix well to make a paste. Gradually stir in the infused coconut milk and heat through, without boiling, until hot.

Pour into small warm cups or ramekins and sprinkle with grated milk chocolate and lime zest. Serve immediately.

Spiced molten puddings

These puddings have become popular on the menus of trendy restaurants. They are very easy to make and can be prepared in advance and cooked just before serving.

Serves 4

- 125g (4oz) unsweetened or 85% (or above) cocoa dark chocolate
- 125g (4oz) unsalted butter, cut into small pieces
- 2 eggs, beaten
- 2 egg yolks
- 4 Tbsp caster sugar
- ½ tsp ground cinnamon
- 2 tsp plain flour
- 4 small pieces white chocolate
- 2 tsp icing sugar
- 1 tsp cocoa powder
- Pouring cream, to serve

Preheat the oven to 230°C/450°F/Gas mark 8. Grease and lightly flour four 150-ml (5-fl oz) pudding basins or ramekins. Break the dark chocolate into pieces and place in a heatproof bowl with the butter. Stand over a pan of gently simmering water and allow to melt, then remove from the water and set aside.

Meanwhile, whisk the eggs, egg yolk and sugar together until thick and creamy. Whisk in the warm melted chocolate, and stir in the cinnamon and flour to make a thick batter.

Divide the mixture between the prepared basins. Push a piece of white chocolate into the centre of each pudding. Place the basins on a baking sheet and cook in the oven for 6–8 minutes until the sides are set but the middle is still wobbly – insert a toothpick carefully into the centre to check that the white chocolate has melted.

Immediately invert the puddings on to warmed serving plates and leave to stand, still in the basins, for 30 seconds before removing. Serve immediately dusted with icing sugar and then cocoa, accompanied with pouring cream.

* * * * * * * * * * *

If you aren't ready to cook the puddings right away, cover them and put in the fridge for up to 24 hours. When you are ready to cook the puddings, make sure they are at room temperature.

Dark chocolate espresso soufflé

The secret of soufflé-making is to be organized. Your wonderful creation needs to be served as soon as it comes out of the oven, before it sinks, so while it's baking, get your serving tools ready!

Serves 6

- 125g (4oz) 70% cocoa dark chocolate
- 2 Tbsp cold water
- 60g (2oz) unsalted butter
- 45g (1½oz) plain flour
- 150ml (5fl oz) whole milk
- 100ml (3½fl oz) cold espresso coffee
- 5 large eggs, separated
- 30g (1oz) caster sugar
- 2 tsp icing sugar
- 1 quantity Coffee cream sauce (see page 175), to serve

Preheat the oven to 190°C/375°F/Gas mark 5 and place a baking sheet in the oven. Grease the base and sides of a 1.5-L (50-fl oz) soufflé dish. Break the chocolate into pieces and place in a small heatproof bowl with the cold water. Stand over a pan of gently simmering water and allow to melt, then remove from the water and set aside.

Meanwhile, melt the butter in a saucepan and blend in the flour. Cook for 1 minute then remove from the heat and gradually blend in the milk and cold coffee. Return to the heat and gently bring to the boil, stirring, until very thick and glossy. Cool for 10 minutes then beat in the melted chocolate, egg yolks and sugar.

In a large grease-free bowl, whisk the egg whites until stiff. Fold a quarter of the egg whites into the chocolate mixture to loosen it, then spoon the chocolate mixture over the remaining whites and fold in carefully.

Turn into the prepared dish. Stand on the preheated baking sheet and bake in the oven for about 40 minutes until risen and firm on the top.

As soon as the soufflé is cooked, dust with icing sugar and serve with hot Coffee cream sauce.

Chocolate risotto

If you want to serve a rich, rib-sticking pudding, this is it. It's really a posh rice pudding, and is very, very chocolatey, and scrummy!

Serves 6–8

- 1.3L (43fl oz) whole milk
- 1 vanilla pod, split
- 60g (2oz) unsalted butter
- 400g (14oz) arborio rice
- 6 Tbsp caster sugar
- 60g (2oz) unsweetened or 85% (or above) cocoa dark chocolate, grated
- 4 Tbsp double cream
- 60g (2oz) plain chocolate chips
- 6 Tbsp mascarpone cheese, to serve
- 1 tsp cocoa powder, to dust

Pour the milk in a saucepan. Bring to the boil. Remove from the heat, add the vanilla pod and leave to infuse for 30 minutes. Discard the pod. In another saucepan, melt the butter and gently stir in the rice until well coated. Add a ladleful of the vanilla milk and cook gently, stirring, until absorbed. Stir in the sugar.

Continue adding small quantities of milk and cooking until it is absorbed, until all the milk is used up and the rice is swollen and tender and the mixture is thick and creamy – this will take about 30 minutes. Stir in the grated chocolate and cream and heat through for a further minute until the chocolate is melted.

To serve, stir in the chocolate chips and pile into warmed serving bowls. Serve each with a spoonful of mascarpone on top and a light dusting of cocoa powder. Serve immediately.

Chocolate and ginger pudding

Steamed pudding is a great comforter on a cold winter's day, and this one is flavoured with the warming power of ginger. Especially delicious when served with my Chocolate custard sauce.

Serves 8

- 90g (3oz) 70% cocoa dark chocolate
- 180g (6oz) unsalted butter
- 180g (6oz) molasses sugar or dark brown sugar
- 3 eggs, beaten
- 2 Tbsp whole milk
- 30g (1oz) preserved ginger, finely chopped
- 180g (6oz) self-raising flour
- 1 tsp ground ginger
- Chocolate custard sauce (see page 174), to serve

Grease a 1.2-L (40-fl oz) pudding basin and place a small disc of baking parchment in the bottom. Break the chocolate into pieces and place in a small heatproof bowl over a pan of gently simmering water and allow to melt, then remove from the water and set aside.

Meanwhile, cream together the butter and sugar in a bowl, until paler, thick and creamy. Gradually whisk in the eggs, milk and melted chocolate, and stir in the chopped ginger.

Sift the flour and ground ginger into the bowl and carefully fold into the chocolate mixture. Spoon into the prepared basin and smooth the top. Top the pudding with a circle of baking parchment, and then cover the top of the pudding basin with a layer of pleated foil. Secure with string.

Half fill a large saucepan with water and bring to the boil. Either place the pudding in a steamer compartment over the saucepan or stand on a trivet in the saucepan. Cover tightly with a lid and steam for 2 hours, topping the water level up as required, until the pudding is risen and firm to the touch – a skewer inserted into the centre of the pudding should come out clean.

To serve, unwrap the pudding and invert on to a warmed serving plate. Serve at once with hot Chocolate custard sauce.

Upside-down banana pudding

Chocolate and bananas go together very well, and in this pudding, the bananas cook to a soft tenderness in a toffee syrup. Choose ripe bananas for best results.

Serves 8

- 225g (7½oz) unsalted butter
- 275g (9oz) light brown sugar
- 3 large ripe bananas
- 4 eggs, beaten
- 1 tsp vanilla extract
- 180g (6oz) self-raising flour
- 15g (½oz) cocoa powder
- ½ tsp ground cinnamon
- Pinch salt
- Chocolate cream sauce (see page 175), to serve

Preheat the oven to 180°C/350°F/Gas mark 4. Melt 100g (3½oz) butter in a saucepan and, when bubbling, add 150g (5oz) of the sugar. Simmer gently for about 3 minutes, stirring occasionally, until syrupy. Pour into the base of a 23-cm (9-in) round cake tin.

Peel the bananas; cut two in half, and then slice through lengthwise. Fan the banana slices in a round over the base of the tin. Set aside. Mash the remaining banana.

In a mixing bowl, cream together the remaining butter and sugar until pale in colour and fluffy in texture. Gradually whisk in the eggs with the vanilla and half the flour. Sieve in the remaining flour, ground cinnamon and salt. Fold in, along with the mashed banana, until well mixed. Pile this mixture on top of the sliced bananas.

Smooth over the top and bake in the oven for 40–45 minutes until lightly golden and firm to the touch. Cool in the tin for 10 minutes, before turning out on to a warmed serving plate and serve immediately, banana-side up, with hot Chocolate cream sauce.

Pear and walnut chocolate crumble

By adding cocoa to a crumble topping you can transform a quite ordinary pudding into something much more sophisticated. This topping also goes well with apricots or a raspberry and apple filling.

Serves 6

- 750g (1½lb) ripe pears
- Finely grated rind and juice of 1 lemon
- 60g (2oz) + 1 Tbsp unbleached caster sugar
- 165g (5½oz) self-raising flour
- 15g (½oz) cocoa powder
- 125g (4oz) butter, cut into small pieces
- 60g (2oz) ground walnuts
- 15g (½oz) walnut pieces
- Chocolate custard sauce (see page 174), to serve

Preheat the oven to 200°C/400°F/Gas mark 6. Peel and core the pears and cut into quarters if small, or small chunks if using large pears. Place in 1.2-L (40-fl oz) oval or round pie dish and sprinkle with the lemon rind, juice and 1 Tbsp sugar. Set aside.

Sieve the flour and cocoa into a bowl and rub in the butter until well combined and the mixture starts to cling together in lumps. Stir in the remaining sugar and the ground walnuts.

Stand the pie dish on a baking tray, and carefully sprinkle the crumble topping evenly over the fruit. Sprinkle with walnut pieces and bake in the oven for about 55 minutes – covering the top with foil if it looks to be darkening too much – until the pears are tender (pierce the pears in the centre of the dish to check). Best served hot with hot Chocolate custard sauce.

Chocolate crêpes with mango

Well worth the effort and guaranteed to impress. Try them with raspberries and raspberry fruit sauce.

Serves 6

- 1 quantity Chocolate cream sauce made with dark chocolate (see page 175)
- 1 quantity mango Fruit sauce (see page 176)
- 125g (4oz) plain flour
- 1 Tbsp cocoa powder
- 30g (1oz) caster sugar
- Pinch salt
- 2 eggs + 2 egg yolks
- 300ml (10fl oz) whole milk
- 75g (2½oz) unsalted butter, melted
- 1 large ripe mango, stoned, peeled and sliced in strips, to serve
- Grated chocolate, to serve

Make the Chocolate cream sauce and Fruit sauce. Set aside.

Sift the flour, cocoa, sugar and salt into a bowl. Make a well in the centre, break in the eggs and add the extra yolks. Add half the milk and gradually work into the flour using a whisk. Beat until smooth, taking care not to overmix.

Add the remaining milk gradually, along with 60g (2oz) butter, whisking all the time. Beat until the ingredients are well combined. Cover and leave in a cool place for 30 minutes. Stir the batter before using.

Lightly brush a 15-cm (6-in) crêpe pan with a little of the remaining melted butter. Pour about 50ml (2fl oz) batter into the pan, tilting the pan to coat the base thinly. Place the pan over a moderate heat and cook for about 1 minute until the crêpe begins to curl away from the pan. Slide a palette knife under the crêpe and flip it over. Cook the underside for a further minute.

Turn out on to a wire rack lined with a clean tea towel and baking parchment. Fold the paper and towel over the crêpe to keep it moist. Continue, making a further 11 crêpes, brushing the pan with melted butter as necessary, and stacking the cooked crêpes between sheets of parchment until ready to serve.

To serve, reheat the Chocolate cream sauce. Place a few strips of mango on each crêpe and fold in half. Arrange two per person on warmed serving plates. Pour over some Chocolate cream sauce and then some Fruit sauce, and decorate with grated chocolate. Serve warm.

Chocolate allspice doughnuts

These doughy, sugar-coated morsels make a real treat for pudding if you serve them with the Chocolate fondue for dipping. A fruity sauce (see page 176) would also work nicely. Great for parties.

Makes 16

- 1 quantity Chocolate fondue (see page 178)
- 180g (6oz) strong plain flour
- 150g (5oz) plain flour
- 30g (1oz) cocoa powder
- ½ tsp salt
- 60g (2oz) unsalted butter
- 180g (6oz) caster sugar
- 2 tsp instant or fast-acting dried yeast
- 200ml (7fl oz) whole milk, slightly warm
- Sunflower oil, for deep-frying
- ½ tsp ground allspice

Make the Chocolate fondue and set aside.

Sift the flours, cocoa powder and salt into a mixing bowl and rub in the butter until the mixture resembles breadcrumbs. Stir in 60g (2oz) sugar and the yeast. Make a well in the centre and gradually blend in the milk to form a soft dough. Cover loosely and stand in a warm place for about an hour or until doubled in size.

Turn the dough on to a lightly-floured surface and knead until smooth. Divide into 16 equal portions and form each into a ball. Push a greased wooden spoon handle through the centre of each, wiggling the spoon to create a hole. Set aside on a lightly-greased tray while heating the oil.

Heat the oil for deep-frying in a large saucepan to 160°C /325°F and cook the doughnuts in batches of five or six for 7–8 minutes, turning occasionally, until they are puffy and crisp. Drain well and keep warm in a shallow dish while cooking all the doughnuts.

Mix the remaining caster sugar with the allspice and then sprinkle over the warm doughnuts, turning them to make sure they are well coated. Serve warm with the Chocolate fondue.

Chocolate Italian bread pudding

Panettone is a sweet, fruity bread from Italy, traditionally eaten at New Year. You could use brioche or sweet cinnamon bread if you prefer.

Serves 6

- 15g (½oz) unsalted butter, softened
- 60g (2oz) candied citrus rind, finely chopped
- 90g (3oz) 70% cocoa dark chocolate, grated
- 450ml (15fl oz) single cream
- 6 thick slices cut from a 500-g (1-lb) panettone (about 350g/12oz)
- 3 eggs, beaten
- 4 Tbsp caster sugar
- Finely grated rind of 1 orange
- 30g (1oz) pine nuts, toasted
- ½ tsp ground cinnamon
- Pouring cream, to serve

Preheat the oven to 180°C/350°F/Gas mark 4. Thickly butter a 1.5-L (50-fl oz) ovenproof gratin dish. Sprinkle the candied rind on the bottom of the dish. Set aside. Place the chocolate and cream in a saucepan. Heat very gently, stirring, until the chocolate melts – do not allow to boil – and then remove from the heat and set aside.

Meanwhile, cut the panettone into small cubes and pack into the prepared dish.

Whisk together the eggs and 2 Tbsp sugar until pale and frothy, and pour over the chocolate cream. Mix well and strain through a sieve. Stir in the orange rind and pour over the bread. Stand for 30 minutes to soak.

Place the gratin dish in a roasting tin and pour sufficient water into the tin to come halfway up the side of the dish. Sprinkle the pudding with pine nuts and bake for 40–45 minutes until the blade of a knife inserted in the centre of the pudding comes out clean. Mix the remaining sugar with the cinnamon and sprinkle over the top of the pudding. Serve hot with pouring cream.

Chocolate orange surprise pudding

This is a delicious recipe I remember from my childhood. Miraculously a rich chocolate sauce appears at the bottom of the dish once the pudding is cooked.

Serves 4–6

- 60g (2oz) butter, softened
- 90g (3oz) light brown sugar
- 2 eggs, separated
- 45g (1½oz) self raising flour
- 1 tsp finely grated orange rind
- 5 tsp cocoa powder
- 350ml (12fl oz) whole milk

Preheat the oven to 180°C/350°F/Gas mark 4. Grease a 1-L (34fl oz) ovenproof dish. In a bowl, cream together the butter and sugar until pale, thick and creamy. Beat in the egg yolks.

Sift the flour and cocoa powder into the bowl and carefully fold into the chocolate mixture along with the orange rind. Gradually stir in the milk to make a smooth, thick batter.

In a grease-free bowl, whisk the egg whites until stiff and fold into the mixture. Spoon into the prepared dish and smooth the top. Stand on a baking sheet and cook for 35–45 minutes until the top is set and spongy to the touch – this pudding will separate into a chocolate sauce layer with a sponge topping. Serve hot with custard.

Chilled desserts

Probably the most diverse recipe section in the book because there's such a variety of tastes and textures. But they do all have one thing in common – lots of chocolate. Another good thing about many of these recipes is that they don't have to be saved for meal times; you could easily have a slice of cheesecake with your morning coffee or a piece of roulade with your afternoon cuppa. Now you know even more about my eating habits!

A lot of people choose chocolate ice cream as their favourite chilled chocolate dessert so I've included an easy method that splits into three chocolate flavours: white, milk and dark; or if you prefer, you can make a bigger batch of your chosen variety. If you're on a dairy-free diet you might like to try the Dark chocolate sorbet instead of ice cream; it's very rich and full of chocolate taste. If you're a real ice-cream lover, then there's a recipe for a chocolate sundae and a trifle.

For the height of chocolate sophistication, there are two recipes definitely worth pointing out: the Three chocolate terrine is one of the simplest and yet most attractive desserts to make, whereas the Chocolate marquise is a classic, dark chocolate recipe for the real connoisseur.

Dark chocolate sorbet

Not quite as rich as ice cream, but this chiller has a big chocolate hit. The sugar syrup means that it melts quite quickly so don't take it out of the freezer too far in advance.

Serves 6

- 1 quantity plain Sugar syrup (see page 174)
- 60g (2oz) cocoa powder
- 1 vanilla pod, split
- Chocolate ginger snaps (see page 183), to serve

★ ☆ ★ ☆ ★ ☆ ★ ☆ ★ ☆ ★

You can make a mocha version of this sorbet by adding 2 tsp instant coffee granules to the syrup when you add the extra cocoa powder. Instead of vanilla you could try using a cinnamon stick, 3 star anise or 4 crushed cardamom pods.

Make the sugar syrup. When the syrup has boiled, sieve the cocoa powder into a heatproof bowl and blend in a little of the syrup to make a paste and then stir the paste into the rest of the syrup until well blended. Add the vanilla pod and set aside to cool completely.

Discard the vanilla pod and, if you have one, churn the mixture in an ice-cream maker until frozen. Store in the freezer until required. Alternatively, pour the mixture into a freezer-proof container and freeze until just beginning to set round the edges, approximately 1–1½ hours. Take out of the freezer and whisk well to break down the ice crystals evenly. Return to the freezer and freeze for a further 1½–2 hours, whisking every 30 minutes, until firm. Cover and store in the freezer until required.

To serve, stand at room temperature for about 5 minutes and scoop into small serving dishes. Serve with Chocolate ginger snaps.

Mocha cream jellies

A jelly might not be the first thing you think of for pudding, unless you're a child, but these creations are well worth considering. The alcohol is optional – you could add a nut syrup instead.

Serves 4

- ½ quantity Chocolate sugar syrup (see page 174)
- 100ml (3½fl oz) espresso coffee, chilled
- 100ml (3½fl oz) single cream
- 4 Tbsp brandy (optional)
- 4 Tbsp cold water
- 5 sheets fine leaf gelatine
- Roasted coffee beans and drinking chocolate, to serve

Make up the Chocolate sugar syrup and set aside to cool. Stir in the coffee, single cream and brandy, if using.

Place 4 Tbsp cold water in a small heatproof bowl. Using a pair of scissors, snip the gelatine into the water. Leave to soak for about 10 minutes. Stand the bowl over a saucepan of simmering water and heat gently until dissolved. Alternatively, heat in the microwave for about 25 seconds on 'high'. Do not allow to boil as this prevents a proper set taking place.

Stir the liquid gelatine into the mocha mixture and pour into four coffee cups or serving dishes. Leave to set in the fridge for at least 2 hours.

To serve, top each with a few roasted coffee beans and a light dusting of drinking chocolate.

Trio of chocolate ices

I'm lucky enough to have an electric ice-cream maker so I can make my own chocolate ice creams quickly. If you haven't got one, here is an easy recipe that makes a fondant-style ice cream that requires no beating.

Serves 6

- 1 quantity plain Sugar syrup (see page 174)
- 75g (2½oz) unsweetened or 85% (or above) cocoa dark chocolate, grated
- 75g (2½oz) milk chocolate, grated
- 75g (2½oz) white chocolate, grated
- Few drops vanilla extract
- 400g (14oz) full-fat soft cheese
- 150ml (5fl oz) double cream

Make the plain Sugar syrup. When it has boiled, divide equally between three heatproof bowls. Stir a different grated chocolate into each bowl, whisking until melted. Set aside to cool. Add a few drops of vanilla extract to the white chocolate syrup.

Once the syrups have cooled, taking each chocolate syrup separately, blend a little syrup into one third of the soft cheese and then whisk in the remaining syrup. Lightly whip the cream and fold one third into each chocolate mixture.

Transfer to three small freezer containers, cover and put in the coldest part of the freezer for at least 4 hours until firmly frozen. Stand at room temperature for about 20 minutes before scooping some of each flavour into individual serving bowls.

White choc and ginger cheesecake

A very simple cheesecake that's rich and satisfying. In order to get a smooth texture, make sure the chocolate is still warm when you add it to the other ingredients.

Serves 10

- 350g (12oz) ginger biscuits, finely crushed
- 1 Tbsp cocoa powder
- 125g (4oz) unsalted butter, melted
- 250g (8oz) white chocolate, broken into pieces
- 300g (10oz) full-fat soft cheese, at room temperature
- 45g (1½oz) preserved ginger in syrup, finely chopped, plus
- 2 Tbsp of the ginger syrup
- 250ml (8fl oz) double cream, at room temperature
- 60g (2oz) plain chocolate, grated

Grease and base-line with baking parchment a deep 23-cm (9-in) spring-release cake tin. Place the crushed biscuits in a bowl and sieve over the cocoa powder. Pour the melted butter over the biscuits and cocoa and bind together. Press onto the base and sides of the tin using the back of a metal spoon. Chill until required.

Place chocolate pieces in a heatproof bowl and melt over a pan of barely simmering water, and set aside. In a large mixing bowl, beat together the soft cheese, chopped ginger, ginger syrup and double cream.

Fold in the warm white chocolate and spoon the mixture over the biscuit base. Smooth the top and chill for 2–3 hours until set.

To serve, release the cheesecake from the tin and place on a serving plate. Sprinkle with grated chocolate and serve.

Chocolate crème brûlée

A much-loved French creation, consisting of a creamy chocolate custard topped with a crunchy, crisp sugar topping. Serve with my Chocolate shortbread to dip (see page 184).

Serves 6

- 600ml (20fl oz) whipping cream
- 60g (2oz) unsweetened or 85% (or above) cocoa dark chocolate, grated
- 1 vanilla pod, split
- 4 egg yolks
- 180g (6oz) caster sugar

Preheat the oven to 150°C/300°F/Gas mark 2. Pour the cream into a saucepan and add the grated chocolate. Heat gently, without boiling, stirring, until hot and the chocolate has melted. Remove from the heat. Add the vanilla pod to the hot cream and leave to infuse for 30 minutes. Discard the pod.

Meanwhile, whisk the egg yolks and 60g (2oz) sugar together in a bowl until thick, pale and creamy. Pour over the chocolate cream, stirring gently until well mixed.

Stand six 150ml (5fl oz) ramekins in a roasting tin and pour the custard mixture slowly into the ramekins, dividing it equally between them. Pour sufficient hot water into the roasting tin to come halfway up the sides of the ramekins.

Bake in the oven for about 1 hour or until set – the blade of a knife inserted into the centre should come out clean when cooked. Remove from the tin and cool completely before chilling for at least 3 hours.

Preheat the grill to its hottest setting. Sprinkle the remaining sugar thickly over the top of each custard. Cook for 3–5 minutes until the sugar turns to caramel. Chill for a further 2 hour before serving.

Three chocolate terrine

Your friends will think this has taken you hours to prepare, when really it's one of the easiest layered desserts I've come across. It's very rich, so serve it in thin slices.

Serves 8

- 125g (4oz) white chocolate
- 125g (4oz) milk chocolate
- 125g (4oz) 70% cocoa dark chocolate
- Few drops vanilla extract
- 450ml (15fl oz) double cream, at room temperature
- 250g (8oz) fresh raspberries, to serve
- 1 quantity raspberry Fruit sauce (see page 176)

Line a 500-g (1-lb) loaf tin with clear food wrap. Break the chocolate into pieces and place each type in a small heatproof bowl and melt over saucepans of barely simmering water. Remove only the white chocolate from the water and add a few drops of vanilla extract. Leave the other two bowls of chocolate on the water, but off the heat, to keep them molten. Set aside.

Lightly whip the cream until just peaking and fold one third into the white chocolate. Transfer to the prepared tin and smooth the surface. Chill for about 30 minutes until firm. While this is chilling, cover the cream and set aside in a cool place – try to avoid chilling it unless it is very warm.

When the white chocolate is set, mix half of the remaining cream with the melted milk chocolate and spread on top of the white chocolate until smooth. Chill once more for about 30 minutes until firm.

Finally, remelt the dark chocolate if necessary. Mix with the remaining cream and spread on top of the milk chocolate layer. Smooth the surface, cover and chill for at least 4 hours until completely set.

To serve, invert the tin on to a serving plate and peel off the food wrap. Arrange fresh raspberries around the edge of the terrine and serve in slices with the raspberry Fruit sauce.

★ ★ ★ ★ ★ ★ ★ ★ ★ ★ ★

You will find the chocolate and cream will stiffen considerably when mixed together, so try and keep the chocolate slightly warm and the cream at room temperature for even mixing and a smooth finished texture.

Iced chocolate cherry trifle

Usually I'm not a great trifle lover, but I have to admit that this one is rather good. If you crave a more traditional version, simply replace the ice cream with chocolate or vanilla custard.

Serves 8

- 1 quantity of Chocolate trifle sponge (see page 181) or six 1-cm (½-in) thick slices ready-made chocolate pound cake
- 500g (1lb) pitted canned cherries in light syrup, drained, reserving 4, or 8 Tbsp syrup (see below)
- 4 Tbsp cherry brandy or Kirsch (optional)
- 1 quantity dark Chocolate cream sauce (see page 175)
- 1 quantity dark chocolate ice cream (see page 134) or 500g (1lb) ready-made chocolate ice cream
- 300ml (10fl oz) whipping cream
- Chocolate decorations of your choice, to decorate

Cut the sponge or cake into bite-size pieces and arrange in the bottom of large glass serving dish. Spoon over the drained cherries and, if using the brandy or Kirsch, spoon over the cherries along with 4 Tbsp reserved juice. If you're omitting the alcohol spoon over 8 Tbsp reserved juice. Cover and chill until required.

Make the dark Chocolate cream sauce. Allow to cool until it is beginning to set, but don't let it set completely otherwise you won't be able to pour it over the trifle.

Scoop the ice cream over the cherries to cover them. Pour the chocolate sauce over the ice cream – it will start to set quickly, so pour it over evenly. Whip the cream until softly peaking and pile on top. Cover and chill for up to 2 hours before serving – it will start to melt if left too long. Decorate and serve as soon as possible (see pages 34–43 for decoration ideas).

Petits pots au chocolat

ne of the all-time classic chocolate
esserts from France. These dense,
ustard-like mousses are rich and
hould really hit the spot if you're
assionate about chocolate.

erves 8

450ml (15fl oz) whole milk
100g (3½oz) unsweetened or
85% (or above) cocoa dark
chocolate, grated
4 egg yolks
60g (2oz) caster sugar
4 Tbsp grated plain chocolate and
8 chocolate coffee dragées to serve

reheat the oven to
60°C/325°F/Gas mark 3. Arrange
ight 100-ml (3½-fl oz) ramekins or
rench custard pots in a roasting tin
nd set aside. Pour the milk into a
aucepan and bring to just below
oiling point. Remove from the heat
nd stir in the chocolate until melted.

Whisk together the egg yolks with the
sugar until pale, thick and creamy.
Pour over the hot chocolate milk,
stirring constantly. Pour the mixture
through a sieve into a heatproof jug.

Divide the chocolate custard mixture
between the ramekins or custard
pots. Pour sufficient hot water into the
roasting tin to come halfway up the
sides of the ramekins. Bake in the
oven for 25–35 minutes, depending
on the size of the ramekin, until just
set but still slightly soft in the centre.
Test by inserting a round bladed knife
in the centre – it should be thickly
coated in the custard to be ready.
Remove from the tin and allow to
cool, then chill for at least 2 hours.

Allow the chocolate pots to stand
at room temperature for about
20 minutes before serving. Sprinkle
with grated chocolate and top with
a chocolate coffee dragée.

Pecan caramel chocolate roulade

A great combination of textures and flavours. You can make the roulade base up in advance, but the roulade is better assembled close to serving as the nut brittle will start to dissolve if refrigerated for too long.

Serves 8

- 6 large eggs, separated
- 150g (5oz) caster sugar
- 60g (2oz) cocoa powder
- 180g (6oz) milk chocolate
- 250g (8oz) mascarpone cheese
- 1 quantity pecan Nut brittle (see page 182), crushed
- 150ml (5fl oz) whipping cream, whipped
- Cocoa powder and icing sugar, to dust

Preheat the oven to 180°C/350°F/Gas mark 4. Grease a 33 x 23-cm (13 x 9-in) Swiss roll tin. Cut a piece of baking parchment 5cm (2in) larger all round than the tin. Press it into the tin, creasing to fit the sides. Cut at the corners of the tin and overlap the cut paper to fit snugly.

In a large bowl, whisk the egg yolks and sugar until very thick and pale. Sieve in the cocoa powder, and using a large metal spoon, fold the ingredients into each other.

In another bowl, whisk the egg whites until just stiff but not dry and fold these into the mixture. Pour into the prepared tin and smooth the surface. Bake in the middle of the oven for 20 minutes until springy to the touch. Take care not to overcook. Leave to cool in the tin – it will sink on cooling!

When the sponge is cool, break the chocolate in pieces and place in a heatproof bowl over a saucepan of barely simmering water until melted. Remove from the water and set aside. Turn the sponge onto a large sheet of baking parchment and peel away the lining paper. Spread the melted chocolate evenly over the surface, then carefully spread over the mascarpone cheese. Sprinkle the Nut brittle on top.

Working quickly, taking hold of one short end of the parchment, use it to gently roll the roulade like a thick Swiss roll. Pull the paper away. The roulade may crack. You should aim to roll the roulade up before the chocolate sets. Put on a serving plate, cover and chill for 30 minutes.

To serve, dust with cocoa and icing sugar and cut into thick slices.

Chocolate velvet slice

This takes a little time to prepare so it's a dessert for a special occasion. It looks impressive, tastes fantastic, and is worth the extra effort.

Serves 10

- Chocolate Swiss roll sponge base (see page 50)
- 125g (4oz) plain chocolate
- 125g (4oz) unsalted butter, cut into small pieces
- 30g (1oz) cocoa powder
- 200ml (7fl oz) double cream
- 2 large eggs
- 125g (4oz) caster sugar
- 60g (2oz) unsweetened or 85% (or above) cocoa dark chocolate
- 60g (2oz) milk chocolate
- Pouring cream or Coffee cream sauce (see page 175), to serve

Line a 1-kg (2-lb) loaf tin with clear food wrap allowing it to overlap the sides and ends. Make and bake the Chocolate Swiss roll sponge but do not roll up; leave as a rectangular sponge base. Remove from the tin and allow to cool on a wire rack. Peel off the paper and trim away the crusts, and then cut the sponge into sufficient pieces to line the bottom and sides of the prepared loaf tin. Carefully press the sponge pieces into the tin. Set aside.

Break the plain chocolate into pieces and place in a heatproof bowl with the butter and melt over a saucepan of barely simmering water. Remove from the water, sieve in the cocoa and mix well. Set aside.

Whisk the eggs and sugar together until pale, thick and creamy. In another bowl, whip the cream until just peaking. Gently mix both the egg and cream into the melted chocolate until well blended. Spoon into the sponge-lined tin and cover with baking parchment. Chill for at least 3 hours.

Break the dark and milk chocolate into pieces and place in separate small heatproof bowls and melt over saucepans of barely simmering water. Remove from the water and set aside.

Invert the terrine on to a small board and remove the food wrap. Drizzle the melted chocolate, alternating, over the top and sides of the terrine. Return to the fridge for 30 minutes.

To serve, carefully cut into slices using a large knife and serve with pouring cream or Coffee cream sauce.

Ultimate chocolate sundae

You can add anything sweet to a sundae and this is my idea of a perfect example. A real treat when you're feeling a bit down in the dumps.

Makes 1

- Large handful of blueberries, washed and dried
- 2 double chocolate cookies, lightly crushed
- 15g (½oz) white chocolate, grated
- 2 scoops Dark chocolate ice cream (see page 134) or ready-made ice cream
- 2 spoonfuls Chocolate custard sauce (see page 174)
- Large swirl of whipped cream
- 15g (½oz) milk chocolate, grated
- Drizzle of Chocolate sugar syrup (see page 174)

Put a few of the blueberries in the bottom of a tall sundae glass and top with some of the crushed cookies and the grated white chocolate. Add a scoop of ice cream and then a spoonful of custard.

Repeat the layers, reserving a few blueberries. Top with a swirl of cream, the milk chocolate, reserved blueberries and finally some Chocolate sugar syrup. Serve immediately and eat using a long-handled spoon. Enjoy!

★ ★ ★ ★ ★ ★ ★ ★ ★ ★ ★

Other good fruits to use in a chocolate sundae are chopped banana, mango, peach or pear, or fresh strawberries and raspberries. For a less calorific version, replace the ice cream with sorbet and top with plain yogurt.

Chocolate marquise

There are many variations of this darkest of chocolate desserts. The chocolate flavour is very intense, so it is best served in thin slices with sweet acid fruits.

Serves 10–12

- 250g (8oz) unsweetened or 85% (or above) cocoa dark chocolate
- 125g (4oz) unsalted butter, softened
- 180g (6oz) icing sugar
- 150ml (5fl oz) double cream, at room temperature
- 1 tsp instant coffee granules dissolved in 2 tsp boiled water, cooled
- 1 Tbsp cocoa powder
- Fresh sweet pineapple and Coffee cream sauce (see page 175), to serve

* * * * * * * * * * * *

Other fruits that go well with this include cape gooseberries (physalis), strawberries and raspberries.

Line a 500-g (1-lb) loaf tin with clear food wrap allowing it to overlap the sides and ends. Break the chocolate in pieces and place in a heatproof bowl over a pan of barely simmering water until melted. Remove from the water and set aside.

Put the butter in a mixing bowl and sieve in the icing sugar. Gradually mix the two together and then beat until soft and smooth. Gradually beat in the melted chocolate. Stir in the cream and coffee mixture.

Pour into the prepared tin and smooth over the top. Cover with clear food wrap and chill for at least 4 hours until firm.

To serve, invert on to a serving plate and remove the food wrap. Stand at room temperature for about 30 minutes before serving. Dredge all over with cocoa powder and accompany with fresh pineapple and Coffee cream sauce.

Chocolate rum 'n' raisin cheesecake

A very rich and cloying baked cheesecake is hard to beat in my opinion. This one has a wonderfully creamy, dense texture that is perfectly complemented by the hint of sweet orange flavour.

Serves 8

- 60g (2oz) seedless raisins
- 2 Tbsp dark rum or freshly squeezed orange juice
- 60g (2oz) unsalted butter
- 180g (6oz) double chocolate chip cookies, crushed
- 500g (1lb) curd cheese
- 1 tsp finely grated orange rind
- 2 eggs, beaten
- 125g (4oz) caster sugar
- 30g (1oz) cocoa powder
- Pouring cream and fresh orange segments, to serve

Preheat the oven to 150°C/300°F/Gas mark 2. Grease and line with baking parchment a 20-cm (8-in) spring-release cake tin. Place the raisins in a small bowl and spoon over the rum or orange juice. Set aside for about an hour to soak and plump up. Meanwhile, melt the butter in a saucepan. Remove from the heat and stir in the crushed cookies. Press the mixture into the base of the tin using the back of a spoon. Chill until required.

In a mixing bowl, beat the curd cheese to soften. Stir in the orange rind and whisk in the eggs and sugar. Sieve in the cocoa powder and carefully stir in along with the soaked raisins and liquid until well mixed.

Transfer to the tin and stand on a baking sheet. Bake for about 1½ hours, covering the top lightly with foil if it begins to brown too quickly, until firm and set. Turn off the heat, leave the oven door ajar, and allow to cool in the oven. Carefully remove from the tin, transfer to a serving plate and chill for 2 hours before serving. Serve with pouring cream and fresh orange segments.

Ice box peanut chocolate torte

I made this one with the younger generation in mind, but I'm sure it'll be popular with everyone. It's fairly sweet so you won't want too much. Take care not to overfreeze the mixture as it will be difficult to cut.

Serves 8

- 125g (4oz) milk chocolate
- 150g (5oz) smooth peanut butter
- 30g (1oz) light brown sugar
- 125g (4oz) full-fat soft cheese, at room temperature
- 250ml (8fl oz) whipping cream, at room temperature
- 20-cm (8-in) round digestive biscuit crumb crust (see tip below)
- 30g (1oz) white chocolate, grated
- 1 tsp cocoa powder

★ ★ ★ ★ ★ ★ ★ ★ ★ ★ ★ ★

To make your own crumb crust, mix 180g (6oz) crushed digestive biscuits with 60g (2oz) melted butter and press into a shallow base-lined 20-cm (8-in) round pie dish. Chill until required.

Break the chocolate into pieces and place in a small heatproof bowl and melt over a saucepan of barely simmering water. Remove from the water and set aside.

Mix the peanut butter and sugar into the milk chocolate, and beat in the soft cheese. Whip the cream until just peaking and whisk into the mixture.

Spoon into the crumb crust. Smooth the top and freeze for 2 hours. Remove from the freezer and stand for 15 minutes at room temperature before serving, sprinkled with grated white chocolate and a dusting of cocoa powder.

Chocolate box gâteau

The method for the chocolate box can be used for round tins or smaller individual cases as well. Try to get an even thickness around the edges in order to support the filling.

Serves 8

- 300g (10oz) plain chocolate
- Chocolate trifle sponge (see page 181)
- 4 Tbsp coconut liqueur or syrup
- 180g (6oz) white chocolate
- 150ml (5fl oz) double cream
- 150ml (5fl oz) coconut milk
- Assorted prepared tropical fruit such as kiwi, mango, pineapple, banana, star fruit, to decorate
- Grated chocolate, to decorate

For the chocolate box, turn upside down an 18-cm (7-in) square cake tin. Mould a double layer of foil around the tin, creasing at corners. Carefully remove the foil and turn the tin right side up. Carefully press the foil 'box' into the tin, smoothing the foil as much as possible. Place a little sticky tape at the top of the middle of each side to secure in place. It should be placed right at the very edge of the foil and fold it down to the edge of the tin. Place in the freezer for 20 minutes.

Break the plain chocolate into pieces and place in a heatproof bowl over a pan of barely simmering water until melted. Remove from the water.

Pour the hot chocolate into the foil-lined tin. Working quickly, tilt the tin to coat the bottom and the sides – you might want to wear gloves to do this as the tin will be very cold. Using a small spatula, spread the chocolate evenly right to the edges of the foil (do not cover the sticky tape), smoothing it into the corners. Chill in the fridge until set.

When the chocolate case is completely set, remove the sticky tape, carefully pull out the foil lining and peel it away from the chocolate. Put the chocolate box on a board. Trim the sponge to fit inside the chocolate box and carefully lower it into the bottom. Spoon the liqueur or syrup over the sponge. Chill until required.

Melt the white chocolate as above and set aside. Whip the cream until just peaking and then whisk in the coconut milk. Fold in the melted white chocolate and then spoon on top of the sponge. Smooth off the top and chill for at least 2 hours until firm.

To serve, decorate the top with a selection of tropical fruit and sprinkle with grated chocolate.

Sweets and treats

I had lots of fun with this section of the book and it made me realise how easy it can be to make sweets. You don't have to worry about sugar thermometers with these recipes, and you'll still achieve perfectly good results.

As well as the classic sweets like fudge, honeycomb and truffles, I've experimented with more exotic ones. Take a look at the Connoisseur Truffles on page 154 to see what I mean. You'll have fun trying them out on your friends – I was amazed at how well these untypical flavours go with dark chocolate – and perhaps you'll be inspired to try other flavours for yourself.

When I was a child, I used to make a refrigerated chocolate cake with my mum. It consisted of crushed digestives bound together with syrup, melted butter and melted chocolate, and set in a square cake tin. Not very healthy, but good as a treat once in a while. I've put in a couple of similar recipes: the Jumble Slice for the kids – they can add anything they want to this – and the Chocolate 'Salami' for the grown ups – an Italian sweetmeat traditionally served with after-dinner coffee. Happy melting!

Connoisseur chocolate truffles

Several of the leading chefs and chocolatiers have experimented with different flavours that go with the darkest of chocolates. Here are two exciting flavours you might like to try on your friends.

Makes 30

- 2 Thai red chillies or a small bunch fresh basil
- 100ml (3½fl oz) double cream
- 30g (1oz) unsalted butter
- 180g (6oz) 85% cocoa dark chocolate
- 200g (7oz) plain chocolate
- Small dark Chocolate curls (see page 35), to decorate

First prepare your chosen flavouring. For the chilli: cut in half and carefully scrape out the seeds. Roughly chop the flesh and place in a bowl. For the basil: wash and pat dry, rip up the leaves and stalk and place in a bowl.

Pour the cream into a small saucepan and add the butter. Heat gently to melt the butter and then pour this over your chosen flavouring and set aside to infuse until cool.

Break the dark chocolate into small pieces and place in a heatproof bowl over a pan of barely simmering water. Allow to melt then remove from the water. Strain the infused cream on to the melted chocolate and mix well. Allow to cool until thick and fudgey. Note: if allowed to set, this mixture will be too hard to pipe.

Meanwhile, melt the plain chocolate as above and remove from the water. Drop small teaspoonfuls of the plain chocolate neatly on a large tray or board lined with baking parchment, and spread lightly to form discs about 4cm (1½in) in diameter. Chill until set.

Transfer the chocolate 'fudge' to a piping bag fitted with a 1-cm (½-in) star nozzle. Pipe a swirl on top of each chocolate disc and chill for at least 30 minutes before serving. Decorate each with a chocolate curl.

No-fuss fudge

Fudge-making can be quite difficult if you don't have a sugar thermometer, but this recipe doesn't need one. You'll end up with a sugary, dense texture that's absolutely delicious.

Makes 64 pieces

- 500g (1lb) milk chocolate
- 397-g (14-oz) can condensed milk
- 250g (8oz) unsweetened desiccated coconut
- ½ tsp ground allspice or cinnamon
- 1 tsp vanilla extract

Grease and line a 20-cm (8-in) square cake tin with baking parchment. Break the chocolate into small pieces and place in a large heatproof bowl. Pour over the condensed milk and stand over a bowl of barely simmering water. Allow to melt then remove from the water and stir until smooth and thick

Mix in the coconut, spice and vanilla extract – the mixture will be very thick. Transfer to the prepared tin, smooth the surface and allow to cool completely. Chill for at least 2 hours until set. Carefully pull out from the tin using the baking parchment and, using a large sharp knife, cut into 64 squares. Store in an airtight container between layers of greaseproof paper and keep in the fridge.

Christmas pudding truffles

Let the children help you make these truffles they can give them as festive treats to their friends. Add a tablespoon or two of rum or brandy for a grown-up version.

Makes 15

- 100g (3½oz) plain chocolate chips
- 250g (8oz) fruit cake
- 100g (3½oz) no-need-to-soak dried figs
- 1 tsp mixed spice
- 60g (2oz) white chocolate chips
- Tubes of red and green ready-made piping icing or coloured fondant, to decorate

Place the plain chocolate chips in a heatproof bowl over a pan of barely simmering water until melted. Remove from the water and set aside.
Put the fruit cake in a blender or food processor with the figs and spice and blend for a few seconds to form a thick paste.

Mix the paste into the melted plain chocolate, allow to cool and then cover and chill for 30 minutes.

Form the chilled mixture into 15 balls and place on a board. Melt the white chocolate as above and spoon a little on top of each ball to resemble brandy sauce. Chill for a further 30 minutes until set.

Either pipe holly leaves and berry shapes on to each truffle, or make the decorations separately with fondant and place on top. Put each truffle in a petit fours case to serve.

Chocolate mint crisps

Pretty little discs of crispy mint chocolate – they look lovely presented in gift-bags and given as a present. Enjoy with a cup of coffee.

Makes 24

- 125g (4oz) granulated sugar
- 125ml (4fl oz) cold water
- 2 tsp peppermint extract
- 250g (8oz) plain chocolate
- Edible silver dragees, to decorate

Put the sugar in a small saucepan with the water. Heat gently, stirring, until the sugar dissolves, then bring to the boil and cook, without stirring, for about 8 minutes until thick and syrupy and just beginning colour – try not to brown the mixture. Remove from the heat and quickly stir in 1 tsp peppermint extract, whisking well. Pour on to a baking sheet lined with baking parchment and tap against the work surface to spread out evenly. Allow to set.

When it is cold, break the minty sugar into small pieces and place in a bowl. Crush with the end of a rolling pin.

Break the chocolate into small pieces and place in a large heatproof bowl and stand over a bowl of barely simmering water. Allow to melt then remove from the water and cool for 10 minutes.

Stir the crushed minty sugar and remaining peppermint extract into the melted chocolate and drop teaspoonfuls of the mixture on to baking sheets lined with baking parchment, smoothing each portion into a round disc. Sprinkle over a few silver dragees before the chocolate sets.

Allow to cool then chill for 1 hour. Peel the sweets off the paper and store in an airtight container betwee layers of greaseproof paper.

Chocolate-covered honeycomb

I love honeycomb – it's crunchy yet chewy texture makes it a very satisfying sweet. Crushed honeycomb can make an interesting topping for ice cream and other chilled desserts.

Makes approx. 36 pieces (depending on size)

- 150g (5oz) granulated sugar
- 2 Tbsp golden syrup
- 2 Tbsp set honey
- 2 tsp bicarbonate of soda
- 400g (14oz) milk chocolate

Grease and line an 18-cm (7-in) square cake tin with baking parchment. Put the sugar in a large saucepan with the syrup and honey. Heat gently, stirring, until the sugar dissolves. Bring to the boil and cook, without stirring, for about 3 minutes until the mixture foams and turns a deep, golden caramel.

Remove from the heat and quickly stir in the bicarbonate of soda. The mixture will immediately foam and bubble up in the saucepan, so quickly pour into the prepared tin while still foaming. Set aside to cool.

When the honeycomb has set, carefully remove from the tin and peel away the paper. Cut into pieces using a large sharp knife – it will shatter so you will end up with different sized and shaped pieces. Arrange the pieces, keeping them spaced apart, on a board lined with baking parchment and set aside.

Break the chocolate into small pieces and place in a large heatproof bowl and stand over a pan of barely simmering water. Allow to melt then remove from the water and cool for 20 minutes.

Using small tongs or two forks, carefully dip the honeycomb pieces into the chocolate to cover them and place back on the parchment. Stand in a cool place to set – only refrigerate if the air temperature is warm and even then, chill for a short time, about 30 minutes, to set the chocolate; after this time the honeycomb may start to dissolve. Any small smashed pieces can be tossed into the remaining melted chocolate and set to make honeycomb clusters.

Peel the sweets off the parchment and store in an airtight container between layers of greaseproof paper.

Chocolate marzipan slice

Homemade marzipan is delicious. It's very easy to make and tastes much richer than anything bought from the store.

Makes 16 slices

- 200g (7oz) ground almonds
- 125g (4oz) caster sugar
- 1 Tbsp cocoa powder
- 1 tsp good-quality vanilla extract
- Few drops pink food colouring
- 1 tsp rose water
- Approx. 5 Tbsp plain Sugar syrup (see page 174)
- Icing sugar, to dust
- 125g (4oz) plain chocolate

Put the ground almonds in a bowl with the caster sugar and mix together. Divide this mix between three small bowls. Stir the cocoa powder into one, the vanilla into another and add a few drops of pink food colouring and the rose water to the third bowl. Bind each together with sufficient Sugar syrup to form a firm pliable paste.

Dust your hands with icing sugar. Roll each piece into a sausage shape approximately 18cm (7in) long and 2.5cm (1in) wide. Lay the pieces neatly one on top of the other, then press gently together to make a thickness of about 4cm (1½in). Wrap in baking parchment and pat gently to square of the sides. Chill until required.

Break the chocolate into small pieces, place in a heatproof bowl and stand over a pan of barely simmering water. Allow to melt then remove from water.

Spread the top of the marzipan with chocolate and chill for 10 minutes until set. Turn the marzipan over, and then spread one side with chocolate and chill until set. Continue in this way until the marzipan is covered. Chill until set.

★ ★ ★ ★ ★ ★ ★ ★ ★ ★

To serve, dip a large, sharp knife in hot, boiled water, dry the blade and use to cut into thin slices. Serve as a sweet treat with coffee or after dinner liqueur.

Chocolate and coconut ice lollies

When the heat's on you can chill out with this sweet chocolatey ice lolly. Easy to make and yummy to eat, you'll hardly be able to wait for them to freeze.

Makes 8

- ½ quantity chocolate sugar syrup (see page 174), cooled
- 200ml (7fl oz) tinned coconut milk
- 60g (2oz) milk chocolate
- 1 Tbsp chocolate flavour sugar strands (vermicelli)
- 1 Tbsp unsweetened desiccated coconut, toasted

Mix the chocolate syrup and coconut milk together and divide between eight 60-ml (4-Tbsp) plastic lolly moulds – if you don't have special moulds, you could use yogurt pots or other small dessert cartons instead. Take care not to over-fill the moulds, because the mixture will expand during freezing. Place in the freezer for at least 4 hours until frozen solid – if you are not using moulds, you'll need to push wooden lolly sticks in to the middle of the lolly mixture just as it starts to freeze. Once the lollies have frozen, dip in hot water for a few seconds then carefully push out from the moulds and place back in the freezer on a board lined with baking parchment.

Break the chocolate into pieces and place in a heatproof bowl over a pan of gently simmering water. Allow to melt, then remove from the water and set aside to cool for 10 minutes. Lightly drizzle the melted chocolate evenly over the lollies and then immediately sprinkle with a few chocolate strands or toasted coconut before the chocolate sets. Either serve straight away or put back in the freezer until you are ready to eat them.

★ ★ ★ ★ ★ ★ ★ ★ ★ ★ ★ ★

For adults, add 4 Tbsp white rum or coconut liqueur to the mixture before freezing.

Jumble slice

You can put almost anything you like in one of these melted chocolate mixtures. Try different types of dried or glacé fruits, and for a less sweet version use continental plain chocolate.

Serves 12

- 150g (5oz) unsalted butter
- 500g (1lb) milk chocolate, broken into small pieces
- 180g (6oz) chocolate chip cookies, crushed into small pieces
- 60g (2oz) glacé cherries, chopped
- 60g (2oz) seedless raisins
- 60g (2oz) mini marshmallows
- 125g (4oz) Maltesers® or honeycomb (see page 160), lightly crushed

Line a 500-g (1-lb) loaf tin with clear food wrap. Place the butter and chocolate in a saucepan over a very low heat, stirring occasionally, until melted. Set aside for 10 minutes.

Meanwhile put the remaining ingredients together in a mixing bowl and stir until well combined.

Pour the melted chocolate over the dry mixture and stir well, making sure that all the pieces are thoroughly coated. Transfer to the prepared tin, press down well, cover loosely and chill for at least 2 hours until firm and set.

Remove from the tin and discard the food wrap. Using a large sharp knife, cut into 12 slices to serve. Keep refrigerated

Salame
al cioccolato

This might sound a little strange at first, but rest assured it's got nothing to do with meat. It is a very rich Italian confection traditionally served at the end of a meal with coffee and liqueur.

Serves 16

- 250g (8oz) 70% cocoa dark chocolate
- 180g (6oz) unsalted butter, cut into pieces
- 60g (2oz) toasted hazelnuts, very finely chopped or ground
- 30g (1oz) candied citrus peel, very finely chopped
- 180g (6oz) crisp amaretti biscuits or almond macaroons, finely crushed
- 30g (1oz) ground almonds
- 15g (½oz) icing sugar

Break the chocolate into small pieces and place in a large heatproof bowl with the butter. Stand over a pan of barely simmering water. Allow to melt then remove from the water and cool for 10 minutes.

Stir the hazelnuts, citrus peel and crushed biscuits into the chocolate and mix well. Leave in a cool place for about 30 minutes to firm up, but not set completely.

Turn the firm chocolate mixture on to a large sheet of baking parchment and form into a salami shape about 25cm (10in) long, with tapering ends. Wrap well in the parchment and chill for at least 4 hours until solid.

Mix the ground almonds and icing sugar together and sieve evenly over a sheet of baking parchment to cover an area the same length as the 'salami'. Unwrap the salami and roll evenly in the sweet almond mixture to coat. Leave to stand for 1 hour before slicing with a large knife, to serve.

Hot chocolate sandwich

If you need a sweet fix then here's the snack for you. Sliced strawberries, mashed raspberries or sliced mango would also be delicious fillings instead of banana.

Serves 1

- 2 slices Pane al cioccolato (see page 108), brioche or other sweet bread, approx. 1-cm (½-in) thick
- 30g (1oz) unsalted butter, softened
- 2 Tbsp Chocolate spread (see page 181)
- 1 large banana, mashed
- 1 small milk chocolate flake bar, crumbled

☆ ★ ☆ ★ ☆ ★ ☆ ★ ☆ ★ ☆ ★

Excellent with Chocolate cream sauce (see page 175) for extra indulgence!

Thickly butter the bread and place buttered side down on a board lined with baking parchment. Spread the unbuttered sides with chocolate spread.

On one slice, carefully spread the mashed banana and sprinkle with chocolate flakes. Peel the other slice of bread off the parchment and gently press, chocolate side down, on top to make a sandwich.

Heat a nonstick ridged griddle or frying pan until hot, and press the sandwich on to the pan for about 2 minutes. Turn over and cook for a further 2 minutes until golden and lightly charred. Drain and serve immediately.

Chocolate ice cream sponge

If you haven't much time, this dessert can be easily put together using ready-made ingredients. I prefer the mixture of white chocolate with blueberries, but you could try other combinations.

Serves 6

- 1 quantity White chocolate ice cream (see page 134) or 500g (1lb) ready-made, good-quality vanilla ice cream
- Chocolate trifle sponge (see page 181) or 19-cm (7-in) ready-made shallow square chocolate cake
- 150g (5oz) blueberries
- 30g (1oz) white chocolate
- 1 tsp cocoa powder

★ ★ ★ ★ ★ ★ ★ ★ ★ ★ ★

If you want to use other fruits in the dessert, make sure you use other berries or cut larger fruit into small pieces. You could use ready-frozen berries; just crush the bigger pieces with a rolling pin before mixing with the ice cream.

Remove the ice cream from the freezer and stand at room temperature until it starts to soften – try to avoid it melting too much.

Meanwhile, carefully line a deep 500-g (1-lb) loaf tin with clear food wrap. Trim the sponge to fit snugly in the bottom of the tin. Cut another piece to fit the top and set aside.

Beat the ice cream to break it up and gently fold in the blueberries. Pack on top of the sponge base and top with the other piece of sponge, pushing down gently. Cover with clear food wrap and freeze for at least 2 hours.

To serve, melt the white chocolate (see page 32). Carefully remove the ice cream sponge from the tin and peel off the food wrap. Drizzle with the white chocolate to serve.

Accompaniments and quick recipes

Chocolate sugar syrup

Makes approx. 600ml (20fl oz)

- 350g (12oz) caster sugar
- 600ml (20fl oz) cold water
- 1 Tbsp cocoa powder

Place the sugar in a saucepan and pour in the water. Heat, stirring, until the sugar dissolves. Raise the heat and bring to the boil. Simmer, without stirring, for 10 minutes.

Remove from the heat. Sieve in the cocoa powder and whisk well. Set aside to cool.

★ ★ ★ ★ ★ ★ ★ ★ ★ ★ ★ ★

For coffee sugar syrup, dissolve 2 tsp instant coffee granules in 1 Tbsp hot, boiled water and stir into the hot syrup. For plain sugar syrup, simply omit the cocoa powder and allow to cool.

Chocolate custard sauce

Makes approx. 600ml (20fl oz)

- 4 level Tbsp cornflour
- 1 Tbsp cocoa powder
- 600ml (20fl oz) whole milk
- 3 Tbsp caster sugar
- 2 egg yolks
- Few drops vanilla extract

In a saucepan, blend the cornflour and cocoa powder with a little milk to make a smooth paste. Stir in the sugar and remaining milk. Heat, stirring, until thick and boiling – use a whisk to help keep it smooth. Cook for 2 minutes. Remove from the heat and cool for 10 minutes.

Stir in the egg yolks and return to the heat. Cook through for 3 minutes, stirring, but without boiling. Add vanilla to taste. To use cold, pour into a heatproof bowl and cover the surface with greaseproof paper to prevent a skin forming. Allow to cool before covering and chilling until required.

★ ★ ★ ★ ★ ★ ★ ★ ★ ★ ★ ★

For a thicker pouring custard, use 1 Tbsp more of cornflour. Omit the cocoa powder for a plain custard.

Chocolate cream sauce

Makes approx. 300ml (10fl oz)

- 180g (6oz) plain chocolate, broken into pieces
- 15g (½oz) unsalted butter
- 6 Tbsp double cream
- 3 Tbsp golden syrup
- Few drops vanilla extract

Put all the ingredients except the vanilla extract in a small heatproof bowl. Stand the bowl over a pan of gently simmering water, and heat gently, stirring occasionally, until all the ingredients have melted together and the sauce is warm. Add a few drops of vanilla extract before serving. Serve warm – the sauce will harden on cooling.

★ ★ ★ ★ ★ ★ ★ ★ ★ ★ ★

For a dark sauce, use unsweetened chocolate. For milk and white chocolate sauces, melt equal quantities of chocolate to double cream – you will not need to add the golden syrup to either sauce.

Coffee cream sauce

Makes approx. 300ml (10fl oz)

- 60g (2oz) unsalted butter
- 125g (4oz) caster sugar
- 125g (4oz) golden syrup
- 2 tsp instant coffee granules dissolved in 1 Tbsp hot, boiled water
- 150ml (5fl oz) double cream

Place the butter, sugar and syrup in a saucepan and heat gently, stirring, until melted and the sugar dissolves. Stir in the coffee and cream and reheat until hot – do not allow to boil. Serve hot or cold.

Fruit sauce
(raspberry and mango flavours)

Makes approx. 550ml (18fl oz)

- ½ quantity plain Sugar syrup (see page 174)
- 250g (8oz) fresh raspberries, washed and prepared or 1 large ripe mango, stoned, peeled and chopped
- 1–2 Tbsp freshly squeezed lemon or lime juice

Make the syrup and add your chosen fruit to the syrup before it cools.

Once cold, transfer to a blender or food processor and blend for a few seconds until smooth. Strain through a nylon sieve to make a smooth sauce. Add lemon or lime juice to taste. Cover and chill until required.

Chocolate pastry

Makes 23-cm (9-in) pastry case or 12 x patty pan tins

- 125g (4oz) plain flour
- 1 Tbsp cocoa powder
- Pinch of salt
- 60g (2oz) caster sugar
- 60g (2oz) unsalted butter
- 1 egg yolk
- Few drops of vanilla extract
- Approx. 1 Tbsp whole milk

Preheat the oven to 200°C/400°F/Gas mark 6. Sieve the flour, cocoa, salt and sugar into a bowl, and rub in the butter to form a mixture that resembles fresh breadcrumbs. Mix in the egg yolk and vanilla extract and bring the mixture together adding milk if necessary, then knead gently to form a firm dough. Wrap and chill for 30 minutes.

Roll out the pastry thinly on a lightly-floured surface to fit a 23-cm (9-in) fluted loose-bottomed flan tin. The pastry is very short so you may find it easier to mould the pastry into the tin. Prick the base all over with a fork and bake in the oven for 15–20 minutes until set and firm to the touch.

White vanilla frosting

Makes sufficient to fill and cover 0-cm (8-in) round, deep cake

400g (14oz) caster sugar
2 egg whites (see note on page 4)
Pinch cream of tartar
Pinch salt
1 tsp vanilla extract

Put all the ingredients except the vanilla extract in a heatproof bowl and whisk to make a thick paste. Place the bowl over a pan of gently simmering water and whisk for 6–7 minutes until thick and peaking.

Remove from the heat and whisk in the vanilla extract. Use this frosting immediately, before it begins to set.

Dark chocolate fudge frosting

Makes sufficient to fill and cover 3-cm (9-in) round cake

300g (10oz) unsweetened or 85% (or above) cocoa dark chocolate, chopped
75g (2½oz) unsalted butter
300g (10oz) icing sugar
75ml (2½fl oz) whole milk, warm

Place the chocolate in a heatproof bowl with the butter and stand over a pan of gently simmering water and allow to melt. Remove from the water and sieve in the icing sugar. Gradually whisk together, adding sufficient milk to form a smooth, spreadable consistency. Use quickly before it sets and becomes difficult to spread.

Chocolate buttercream

**Makes sufficient to fill and top
19-cm (7-in) round cake or top
12 muffins or fill a Swiss roll**

- 90g (3oz) unsalted butter, softened
- 180g (6oz) icing sugar
- 1 Tbsp cocoa powder dissolved in
  2 Tbsp boiled water, cooled

Put the butter in a bowl and
gradually sieve in the icing
sugar, beating well between
each addition, until smooth and
creamy. Stir in the chocolate liquid
and beat to soften the mixture to a
spreadable consistency.

* * * * * * * * * * *

*Add a few drops of vanilla extract
or ½ tsp grated orange rind, if liked
or replace 1 tsp cocoa powder with
1 tsp instant coffee granules for a
mocha buttercream.*

Chocolate fondue

Serves 6

- 250g (8oz) plain chocolate, broken
  into pieces
- 250ml (8fl oz) double cream
- 4 Tbsp dark rum or freshly
  squeezed orange juice
- 2 Tbsp dark brown sugar

Place the chocolate in a fondue pot
or small saucepan. Pour in the cream,
rum or juice, and add the sugar.

Place over a gentle heat, and cook,
stirring, until melted and well blended.

Either transfer to the fondue stand and
keep warm over the lit spirit burner,
or warm over a low heat on the
cooker when required to serve.

* * * * * * * * * * *

*The cocoa content of the chocolate
used will determine the sweetness of
the chocolate cream, so choose a
chocolate according to taste. This
recipe also works with milk and white
chocolate, but you will not need to
add the sugar.*

Glossy
chocolate cream

**Makes sufficient to cover
75-cm (10-in) round cake**

- 200g (7oz) plain chocolate, broken
  into pieces
  250ml (8fl oz) double cream, at
  room temperature

Place the chocolate pieces in a
heatproof bowl over a pan of gently
simmering water and allow to melt.
Remove from the water and set aside
to cool until slightly warm – about
10 minutes.

While whisking the chocolate,
gradually pour in the cream,
whisking until thickly whipped and
glossy. The mixture is now ready for
spreading or piping. Once chilled
the mixture will set firm.

* * * * * * * * * * *

*The cocoa content of the chocolate
used will determine the sweetness
of the chocolate cream, so choose
a chocolate according to taste.
This recipe also works with milk
and white chocolate.*

Chocolate
glacé icing

**Makes sufficient to cover
10–12 cupcakes or muffins**

180g (6oz) icing sugar
1 Tbsp cocoa powder
Approx. 5–6 tsp warm,
boiled water

Sieve the icing sugar and cocoa
into a bowl and gradually add
sufficient water to make a smooth
spreadable icing.

* * * * * * * * * * *

*Add a few drops of vanilla extract
for extra flavour. Other flavours to
add are peppermint essence, 1 tsp
instant coffee granules dissolved in
the water or ½ tsp finely grated
orange rind.*

Rich hot chocolate drink

Serves 1

- 30g (1oz) plain chocolate, grated
- 200ml (7fl oz) whole milk
- 2 small cinnamon sticks
- 1 strip pared orange rind
- 2 Tbsp milk Chocolate spread (see page 181)

Put the grated chocolate in a small saucepan and pour over the milk. Add one cinnamon stick and orange rind. Heat very gently until the chocolate melts, then stir in the Chocolate spread and heat until melted. Bring to just below boiling and turn off the heat. Stand for 5 minutes before straining into a mug. Serve with a cinnamon stick as a stirrer.

White chocolate toddy

Serves 1

- 60g (2oz) white chocolate, grated
- 2 Tbsp double cream
- 180ml (6fl oz) whole milk
- ¼ tsp ground nutmeg
- Few drops vanilla extract

Put the grated chocolate in a small saucepan and pour over the cream and milk. Add half the nutmeg. Heat very gently, without boiling, until the chocolate melts. Continue to heat until piping hot but not boiling. Remove from the heat and add a few drops of vanilla extract. Pour into a mug and serve sprinkled with the remaining nutmeg.

Chocolate
trifle sponge

**Makes sufficient sponge for a
large trifle**

- 2 large eggs
- 60g (2oz) caster sugar
- 30g (1oz) plain flour
- 15g (½oz) cocoa powder
- 2 tsp cornflour
- 30g (1oz) butter, melted

Preheat the oven to
180°C/350°F/Gas mark 4. Grease
and line with baking parchment a
20-cm (8-in) square cake tin. Put the
eggs and sugar in a large clean bowl
and stand over a large bowl of hot
water. Whisk until thick, pale and
creamy – about 5 minutes. Remove
from the bowl of water and continue
to whisk for a further 3 minutes. You
should be able to leave a trail from
a spoon in the mixture when it is
whisked sufficiently.

Sieve in the flour, cocoa and
cornflour. Pour the melted butter
around the edge of the mixture and
carefully fold the mixture together
using a large metal spoon. Pour into
the prepared tin and bake in the
oven for 20–25 minutes until well
risen and just firm to the touch.
Remove from the tin and cool on
a wire rack.

Chocolate
spread

Makes 300g (10oz)

- 125g (4oz) milk or plain chocolate,
  broken into pieces
- 60g (2oz) unsalted butter
- 3 Tbsp golden syrup
- 3 Tbsp double cream

Place all the ingredients in a
saucepan and heat very gently,
stirring, until melted together, then
remove from the heat and allow
to cool.

Transfer to a sealable container
and store in the refrigerator for up
to 2 weeks.

Chocolate and vanilla pinwheels

Makes 18

- 125g (4oz) butter, softened
- 60g (2oz) caster sugar
- 1 egg, beaten
- 1 tsp vanilla extract
- 200g (7oz) plain flour
- 15g (1/2oz) cocoa

Cream the butter and sugar together until pale and creamy. Beat in the egg and vanilla. Sieve in the flour and mix to form a soft dough. Wrap half the dough and chill until required. Sieve the cocoa over the remaining dough and mix in thoroughly. Wrap and chill for 1 hour.

On a lightly floured surface roll each dough to form an oblong 25 x 20cm (10 x 8in), and place on top of each other. Roll up tightly from the short end. Wrap and chill for 30 minutes.

Preheat the oven to 190°C/375°F/Gas mark 5. Trim away the ends of the roll and slice thinly to make 18 rounds. Place a little distance apart on baking sheets lined with baking parchment and bake for 10–12 minutes until pale golden and set. Transfer to a wire rack to cool.

Nut brittle

Makes approx. 200g (7oz)

- 180g (6oz) granulated sugar
- 100ml (3½fl oz) cold water
- 60g (2oz) unsalted roasted nuts such as pecans, hazelnuts, almonds or peanuts, chopped

Put the sugar in a saucepan with the water and heat gently until dissolved. Raise the heat and boil rapidly, without stirring, for 7–8 minutes until the syrup turns light golden brown.

Remove from the heat and dip the base of the saucepan briefly in cold water to prevent the caramel from cooking further. Working quickly, pour prepared caramel on to an oiled baking sheet and scatter over chopped nuts. Allow to cool.

When cold, lightly crush with a rolling pin and use as shards to decorate desserts such as trifles or cream-topped pies; or crush finer and use to mix into creams for fillings.

Maple chocolate smoothie

Serves 2

2 scoops Dark chocolate ice cream (see page 134)
300ml (10fl oz) whole milk
2 Tbsp maple syrup
Few drops vanilla extract
2 scoops Milk chocolate ice cream (see page 134)
Chocolate cream sauce (see page 175), to drizzle
2 tsp white chocolate, grated

Put the Dark chocolate ice cream, milk, maple syrup and a few drops vanilla extract in a blender and blend for a few seconds until smooth.

Immediately pour into two tall glasses. Add a scoop of Milk chocolate ice cream to each glass. Drizzle with sauce and sprinkle with grated chocolate. Serve immediately.

Chocolate ginger snaps

Makes 24

60g (2oz) unsalted butter
60g (2oz) unbleached granulated or demerara sugar
60g (2oz) golden syrup
45g (1½oz) plain flour
15g (½oz) cocoa powder
½ tsp ground ginger

Preheat the oven to 180°C/350°F/Gas mark 4. Line two large baking sheets with baking parchment. Put the butter, sugar and syrup into a saucepan and heat gently, stirring, until the butter melts and the sugar dissolves. Remove from the heat and cool for 10 minutes.

Sieve in the flour, cocoa and ginger and mix well. Drop small teaspoonfuls of the mixture on to the baking sheets, spaced about 7.5cm (3in) apart. Bake for 7–8 minutes until bubbling and spread. Leave to cool on the sheets, then remove and store between layers of greaseproof paper in an airtight container for up to 1 week.

Chocolate shortbread

Makes 24 fingers

- 250g (8oz) butter, softened
- 125g (4oz) unbleached caster sugar
- 320g (10½oz) plain flour
- ½ tsp salt
- 30g (1oz) cocoa powder

★ ★ ★ ★ ★ ★ ★ ★ ★ ★ ★ ★

Dredge with a little caster sugar and a light dusting of cocoa powder to serve, if liked.

Preheat the oven to 160°C/325°F/Gas mark 3. In a bowl, beat the butter and sugar together until soft and creamy. Add the flour and salt and sieve over the cocoa powder. Carefully mix together and then beat until well combined.

Press into an 18 x 28-cm (7 x 11-in) oblong cake tin. Prick all over with a fork and bake in the oven for about 1 hour until firm. Cut into 24 fingers while warm and allow to cool in the tin.

Bibliography

Coady, Chantal: **The Connoisseur's Guide to Chocolate** (Apple, 2006)

Davidson, Alan: **The Oxford Companion of Food** (Oxford University Press, 1999)

McGee, Harold: **McGee On Food and Cooking** (Hodder & Stoughton, 2004)

Smith, Andrew. F: **The Oxford Encyclopaedia of Food and Drink in America** (Oxford University Press, 2004)

Larousse Gastronomique (Paul Hamlyn, 1989)

About the author

Kathryn Hawkins is an experienced cookery writer and food stylist. She has worked on several women's magazines as part of their full-time staff and, since 1992, as a freelancer. A former cookery editor of the bestselling weekly magazine *Woman's Own*, Kathryn moved from London to Crieff in central Scotland in 2004, where she runs a guest house.

Kathryn enjoys using local produce and is passionate about the quality and freshness of food on her doorstep. She writes on a wide range of cookery subjects and has a particular interest in cakes and baking, regional dishes, diet and healthy eating. She is a member of the Guild of Food Writers and the Slow Food movement.

As well as writing, Kathryn has prepared food for hundreds of photographs in advertisements, on food packaging, menus, and in magazines and books; she also teaches privately on a variety of subjects.

Top chocolatiers of the world

With specialist chocolate shops and delicatessens selling homemade chocolates for our delectation just about everywhere you turn these days, I thought it might be useful to list some of the most famous producers of the world's finest chocolate. It would be a very long list to include them all, so this is only a taster. You'll be able to add your own favourites as you develop your chocolate palate.

MC means that they have been given the title master chocolatier.

AUSTRIA

Altman & Kühne
www.feinspitz.com/ak/
L. Heiner
www.heiner.co.at

BELGIUM

Mary
www.marychoc.com
Wittamer
www.wittamer.com

CANADA

Bernard Callebaut
www.bernardcallebaut.com

FRANCE

Jean-Paul Hévin (MC)
www.jphevin.com
La Maison du Chocolat (MC)
www.lamaisonduchocolat.com
Michel Chaudin (MC)
149 Rue de l'Université, 75007 Paris
Pierre Hermé (MC)
www.pierreherme.com
Richart (MC)
www.richart-chocolates.com

GERMANY

Dreimeister
www.dreimeister.de
Fassbender
www.fassbender.de

ITALY

Amedei
www.amedei.it
De Bondt (MC)
Via Turati 22 (Corte San Domenico)
56125 Pisa, Italy

LUXEMBOURG

Oberweis
www.oberweis.lu

SPAIN

Baixas
Calaf 9–11, 08021 Barcelona
Fransico Torreblanca
www.torreblanca.net

SWEDEN

Hovby No 9
www.hovbyno9.se
Robert E's Choklad
www.robertes-choklad.com

SWITZERLAND

Camille Bloch
www.camillebloch.ch
Dudle
Weggisgasse 34, Lucerne CH-6004,
Switzerland

UNITED KINGDOM

L'Artisan du Chocolat
www.artisanduchocolat.com
The Chocolate Society
www.chocolate.co.uk
Plaisir du Chocolat
www.plaisirduchocolat.com
Rococo
www.rococochocolates.com

UNITED STATES OF AMERICA

Fran's Chocolates
www.franschocolates.com
Michael Recchiuti
www.recchiuti.com
Richard Donnelly Fine Chocolates
www.donnellychocolates.com
Woodhouse Chocolat
www.woodhousechocolate.com

Index